T0360477

Exploring Public-Private Partnerships in Singapore

This book looks at what drives effective management of public-private partnerships (PPPs). It examines widely cited Singaporean cases pertaining to successful PPPs as well as those in failure (and subsequently contracted back in the public-sector provision) in diverse areas of public service, such as water services, educational services, trade and logistical data services, residential services, acquisition and maintenance of military systems, research and development services, infrastructure, and sport services.

The book begins each case with an overview (e.g., project goals (motivators), types of PPPs, stakeholders, time period, assigned budget, and capital planning) and then specifically discusses critical success factors and/or risk factors pertaining to the decisions to proceed with ongoing PPPs or to return to self-operation (in-house public production) of services later, respectively. The book concludes with a discussion of lessons learned from Singaporean cases and contexts of PPPs and suggests more feasible strategies and conditions toward successful collaborative governance between public agencies and private counterparts for the new century.

This book will appeal especially to public policymakers.

Soojin Kim is Assistant Professor of the Public Policy and Global Affairs Programme, School of Social Sciences, Nanyang Technological University, Singapore. She earned her PhD in the School of Public Affairs and Administration, Rutgers, The State University of New Jersey, Newark Campus, in May 2015. Her research and teaching interests focus on public budgeting and financial management, contracting out, public-private partnerships, institutional arrangements in policy choices, and mixed methods research design.

Kai Xiang Kwa is currently a PhD candidate at the School of Social Sciences at Nanyang Technological University, Singapore. His research interests include: public administration (PA) and public policy (PP) in Singapore and China; public service motivation (PSM) in Singapore and China; politics, media and culture in PA and PP; mixed methods, quantitative and qualitative research methods in PA and PP.

Routledge Focus on Public Governance in Asia
Series Editors:
Hong Liu
Nanyang Technological University, Singapore
Wenxuan Yu
Xiamen University, China

Focusing on new governance challenges, practices and experiences in and about a globalizing Asia, particularly East Asia and Southeast Asia, this focus series invites upcoming and established researchers all over the world to succinctly and comprehensively discuss important public administration and policy themes such as government administrative reform, public budgeting reform, government crisis management, public private partnership, science and technology policy, technology-enabled public service delivery, public health and aging, talent management, and anticorruption across Asian countries. The book series presents compact and concise content under 50,000 words long which have significant theoretical contributions to the governance theory with an Asian perspective and practical implications for administration and policy reform and innovation.

Translation and the Sustainable Development Goals
Cultural Contexts in China and Japan
Meng Ji and Chris G. Pope

The Two Sides of Korean Administrative Culture
Competitiveness or Collectivism?
Tobin Im

Political Economic Perspectives of China's Belt and Road Initiative
Reshaping Regional Integration
Christian Ploberger

Exploring Public-Private Partnerships in Singapore
The Success-Failure Continuum
Soojin Kim and Kai Xiang Kwa

For more information about this series, please visit www.routledge.com/ Routledge-Focus-on-Public-Governance-in-Asia/book-series/RFPGA

Exploring Public-Private Partnerships in Singapore

The Success-Failure Continuum

**Soojin Kim and
Kai Xiang Kwa**

Routledge
Taylor & Francis Group

LONDON AND NEW YORK

First published 2020
by Routledge
2 Park Square, Milton Park, Abingdon, Oxon OX14 4RN

and by Routledge
52 Vanderbilt Avenue, New York, NY 10017

Routledge is an imprint of the Taylor & Francis Group, an informa business

British Library Cataloguing-in-Publication Data
A catalogue record for this book is available from the British Library

Library of Congress Cataloging-in-Publication Data
Names: Kim, Soojin, author. | Kwa, Kai Xiang, author.
Title: Exploring public-private partnerships in Singapore : the
    success-failure continuum / Soojin Kim, Kai Xiang Kwa.
Description: Abingdon, Oxon ; New York, NY : Routledge, 2020. |
    Series: Routledge focus on public governance in Asia | Includes
    bibliographical references and index.
Identifiers: LCCN 2019043710 (print) | LCCN 2019043711 (ebook)
Subjects: LCSH: Public-private sector cooperation—Singapore—
    Management. | Public-private sector cooperation—Singapore—
    Case studies.
Classification: LCC HD3872.S56 K55 2020 (print) | LCC HD3872.S56
    (ebook) | DDC 338.8/7—dc23
LC record available at https://lccn.loc.gov/2019043710
LC ebook record available at https://lccn.loc.gov/2019043711

ISBN: 978-0-367-25945-7 (hbk)
ISBN: 978-0-429-29070-1 (ebk)

Typeset in Times New Roman
by Apex CoVantage, LLC

Contents

Figures

Tables

Acknowledgments

This work was supported by the Ministry of Education of the Republic of Korea and the National Research Foundation of Korea (NRF-2018S1A3A2075609); and HASS Incentive Scheme for the Development of Competitive Research Grant (No. M4082261.SS0) from Nanyang Technological University, Singapore.

Abbreviations

A*STAR	Agency for Science, Technology and Research
ARTC	Advanced Remanufacturing Technology Centre
BBO	Buy-Build-Operate
BDO	Buy/Lease-Develop-Operate
BOO	Build-Own-Operate
BOOT	Build-Own-Operate-Transfer
BOT	Build-Operate-Transfer
BTO	Build-Transfer-Operate
CHAS	Community Health Assist Scheme
COI	Committee of Inquiry
CP2M	Centre for Public Project Management
CPIB	Corrupt Practices Investigations Bureau
CRFs	Critical risk factors
CSCG	CS Construction and Geotechnic
CSFs	Critical success factors
DB	Design-Build
DBFO	Design-Build-Finance-Operate
DBM	Design-Build-Maintain
DBO	Design-Build-Operate
DBOM	Design-Build-Operate-Maintain
DBOO	Design, Build, Own and Operate
DBOT	Design-Build-Operate-Turnover
DBSS	Design, Build and Sell Scheme
DBW	Design-Build-Warranty
ECC	Emergency Care Collaboration
EOI	Expressions of interest
GeBIZ	Government Electronic Business
GPE	Government Procuring Entity
HCI	Human Capital Index
HDB	Housing and Development Board

HPB	Health Promotion Board, Singapore
ICT	Information and communication technology
IDA	Info-communications Development Authority of Singapore
IT	Information Technology
ITE	Institute of Technical Education
ITT	Invitation to tender
LBO	Lease-Build-Operate
LTA	Land Transport Authority
MINDEF	Ministry of Defence, Singapore
MOF	Ministry of Finance, Singapore
MOH	Ministry of Health, Singapore
MRT	Mass Rapid Transit
NEA	National Environment Agency
NetCo	Network Company
NLB	National Library Board, Singapore
NS	National Service
NUS	National University of Singapore
OECD	Organization for Economic Cooperation and Development
OpCo	Operating Company
P2P	Peer-to-Peer
PFI	Private Finance Initiative
PPI	Private Participation in Infrastructure
PPPs	Public-Private Partnerships
PUB	Public Utilities Board
RFP	Request for Proposal
ROI	Return on investment
RSAF	Republic of Singapore Air Force
SAF	Singapore Armed Forces
SCDF	Singapore Civil Defence Force
SMRT	Singapore Mass Rapid Transit
SMU	Singapore Management University
SPF	Singapore Police Force
SSC	Singapore Sports Council
VFM	Value for Money

1 Introduction

Why Public-Private Partnerships (PPPs)?

1 The historical background of PPPs

Over the past few decades, spurred on by cost-efficient and business-like government reforms (e.g., Reinventing Government and New Public Management) and the change in demographic structure (e.g., aging population), many developed and developing countries have continued to pursue their production and delivery of public goods and services by awarding contracts to the private sector. Such change in governance, for example, using privatization or contracting-out, has aimed to achieve cost savings and ensure government responsibility toward the modern welfare state without compromising public policy goals and heightened citizens' needs for more and better services. Scholars and practitioners have described this global phenomenon using diverse terms like 'third-party governance' (Salamon, 1981), 'government by proxy' (Kettl, 1988), 'hollow state' (Milward & Provan, 2000), and 'contracting regime' (Smith & Lipsky, 1993) – all of which encompass the broadening of new public management strategies in the context of contractual relationships between public and nongovernment organizations outside the public sector (Kim, 2015).

In recent decades, this line of discussion has been extended to public-private partnerships (hereafter, PPPs), which are based on long-term cooperation and mutual understanding between the public- and private-sector actors. A huge volume of literature, particularly evidence-based research on PPPs, has flourished in the area of public administration and policy since the late 1990s (Leigland, 2018). Scholars have started to call PPPs 'hybrid forms' (Koppell, 2003), 'third way governments' (Hodge & Greve, 2007), and 'cross-sectoral collaboration' (Brinkerhoff & Brinkerhoff, 2011).

In history, the concept of using private capital to provide public services, especially public facilities (i.e., repairing the roads, paying debt by charging bridge tolls), seems to be quite old (Yescombe, 2007). Western countries, as pioneers of this practice, started to allow private firms to enter the public sphere in the 18th century (Gunawansa, 2010; Kumaraswamy & Morris, 2002). For example, in France, the construction of canals with private capital began through the concession type of practice (e.g., charging toll fees to pay back the initial investment) (Yescombe, 2007, p. 5). Likewise, most of London's bridges and tunnels were financed by private investors, and the private counterparts were allowed to charge so-called public service fees to bridge users. The Brooklyn Bridge in New York was also built in the same way. This was to help finance the building of public facilities and to substantially lower debt burdens shouldered by governments.

PPPs have started to elicit a great deal of attention globally in the scholarship as well as the practice since the United Kingdom (UK) first introduced PPPs at the national level in 1992 (Gunawansa, 2010; Lam, 2004; Leigland, 2018). As an innovative strategy for effectively delivering public services to the people, the UK government executed the Private Finance Initiative (PFI), which enabled the government to use alternative sources of (private) funds for infrastructure. By April 2003, about 560 PFI contracts had been executed, which made up more than 10 percent of the total investment in the UK public sector in 2003–2004 (Corner, 2005, p. 44). In response to the UK's successful PPP operations, other European countries (e.g., PPPs were first introduced in France in 2004) and the United States have increasingly relied on PPPs, not only to finance their infrastructure building/renovation but also to enhance urban renewal and local economic development in the long term (Hodge & Greve, 2007; Osborne, 2001).

Later in the 20th century, Asian countries have not been an exception to this trend. This is because many countries in the Asian and Pacific region pursued greater efficiency (associated with rapid economic growth) through private involvement in public-sector works and subsequently recovered citizens' trust in government through such strategic public management. As a result, PPPs initially tended to appear in the area of large-scale urban infrastructure and related services, mostly in terms of public transport infrastructure projects such as highways (express lanes), inter-state bridges, airports, harbors, and tunnels (Ni, 2012; Velotti, Botti, & Vesci, 2012). However, to date, PPPs have spread to other industries (service areas), including information technology (IT), medical services, residential services, military/defense, sport stadiums and sewerage (recycled water) treatment, to mention a few.

Notably, it has been argued that PPPs are different from the traditional bureaucratic public service delivery method (including competitive tendering) or privatization (Hodge & Greve, 2007). Rather, PPPs seem to go beyond the traditional government purchase of goods and services through procurement/contracting-out in that the operator or service provider (and its financiers) in the private sector has specific roles even in the design, construction (including renovation), and financing stages in addition to their operational roles (Bovaird, 2004; Hodge & Greve, 2005; Wang & Zhao, 2014). To manage PPPs successfully, consistent intersectoral collaborations between the two sector bodies are required for promising long-term contractual relationships (i.e., concession periods)[1] (Forrer, Kee, Newcomer, & Boyer, 2010).

According to Forrer and his colleagues (2010), in a traditional competitive approach, governments tend to dictate the terms and conditions of service production and delivery, and private vendors are expected to comply with the contractual specifications. However, in a PPP project, both government agencies and private partners are actively engaged in the pre- and post-award negotiations to determine how the good or service might be provided (Forrer et al., 2010, pp. 476–477). In other words, under the PPPs, two or more stakeholders (partners per se), at least one of which is a public entity and one a private entity (a private company or consortium), not only proceed with joint decision-making but also share risks (and costs and resources related to the products and services if necessary), responsibilities for the outcome, and further returns on investment in the long-term relationship (Evans & Bowman, 2005; Hodge & Greve, 2007; Marques & Berg, 2011; Ni, 2012). However, it should be noted that as in the PPP Handbook developed by the Ministry of Finance (MOF), Singapore, governments utilizing PPPs are allowed to invite private-sector entities to finance and develop infrastructure projects without losing the state control over the regulatory aspects of service delivery, including the pricing of services provided by the infrastructure facility (MOF, 2012, p. 4). This is reminiscent of Baker's (2016) argument that "[a] PPP is a hybrid structure that lies between the traditional provision of public goods and services by the government and pure privatization" (p. 433).

Although the public and private partners are expected to work together toward a common goal (e.g., providing better performance of targeted services to fulfill citizens' expectations) in the PPP relationships, each sector actor needs to play an independent, significant role in improving public services or creating innovation. Under PPPs, a public entity is typically in charge of specifying the outputs or services required, whereas a private company or consortium (known as a project developer) should be responsible for financing, designing, construction, operation and maintenance of a facility (service) (Gunawansa, 2010; MOF, 2012). More specifically, in the words of Ni (2012),

[t]he public sector contributes social responsibility, public accountability, political responsiveness, environmental awareness, local knowledge, and job creation and equity concerns; while the private sector encompasses efficiency, access to finance and resources, knowledge of technologies, innovativeness and nimbleness, and entrepreneurism.

(p. 256)

2   Global trends of PPPs

As a result of the widespread popularity of PPPs around the world in the 1990s, diverse public infrastructure projects, such as building and renewing highways, roads, tunnels, sewerage (recycled water) treatment, harbors, airports, or sport stadiums, have been earmarked as a typical example of PPPs. In particular, as noted above, since the UK's Private Finance Initiative (PFI) in 1992, many European countries have introduced the number of PPPs considerably for the provision of diverse public services, beyond mere infrastructure-related projects.

According to one data portal of the European Investment Bank (2017) dealing with 28 EU countries, Turkey, and countries of the Western Balkans region (1990–2016), it was found that aside from the transport infrastructure projects, other service areas, including environment, education, public order and safety, defense, healthcare, housing, and telecommunications, have been provided for in the form of PPPs. As Table 1.1 shows, in terms of total PPP investments in European countries, as predicted, the transport sector has been the most prolific. Interestingly, healthcare, education, and the environment sectors have a relatively higher portion of total PPP investment value as compared with other sectors.

From a broader perspective, other countries in Asia, Latin America, the Middle East, and Africa have not been spared from such a worldwide

Table 1.1 Breakdown of Total PPP Value by Sector

Sector	Investment (billion EUR)
Transport	211.992
Environment	24.308
Education	35.997
Public order and safety	12.954
Recreation and culture	6.807
General public services	7.29
Defense	18.271
Healthcare	50.717
Housing and community services	7.456
RDI (Research, development, and innovation)	0.16
Telcos (Telecommunications companies)	7.291

Source: Table was made based on data adapted from European Investment Bank. (2017). Total value of European PPP projects by sector – all countries and number of European PPP projects by sector. European PPP Expertise Centre (EPEC) Data Portal. Retrieved August 12, 2019, from https://data.eib.org/epec

governance change toward PPPs. The World Bank's (n.d.) Private Participation in Infrastructure (PPI) Project database has dealt with over 6,400 PPP projects in approximately 130 low- and mid-income countries. This database has recorded not only the number and investment value of PPI projects (aggregated ones and divided ones by region or sector) but also their historical changes over the period 1990–2018 in six regions of the world: (1) East Asia and Pacific, (2) Europe and Central Asia, (3) Latin America and the Caribbean, (4) Middle East and North Africa, (5) South Asia, and (6) Sub-Saharan Africa (see Table 1.2, Table 1.3, and Figure 1.1 below).

According to Table 1.2, among many countries having transitional economies, with respect to the number of PPI projects, Latin America and the Caribbean region are ranked first; East Asia and Pacific are ranked second; and South Asia is ranked third. In addition, Table 1.3 shows the total US dollar PPI investment by sector. As opposed to expectations, the private

Table 1.2 Breakdown of PPI Projects by Region

Region	Number of PPI Projects
East Asia and Pacific	2,491
Europe and Central Asia	1,206
Latin America and the Caribbean	3,100
Middle East and North Africa	216
South Asia	1,427
Sub-Saharan Africa	590

Source: Table 1.2 was made based on data adapted from World Bank (n.d.). Private participation in infrastructure (PPI) project database. Retrieved June 30, 2019, from https://ppi.worldbank.org/en/ppidata

Table 1.3 Breakdown of Total PPI Investment by Sector

Sector	Investment (million US$)
Energy	963,246
Information and communication technology (ICT)	123,590
Transport	627,284
Water and sewerage	76,515

Source: Table 1.3 was made based on data adapted from World Bank (n.d.). Private participation in infrastructure (PPI) project database. Retrieved June 30, 2019, from https://ppi.worldbank.org/en/ppidata

Note: Energy represents electricity and natural gas. Transport represents airports, ports, railways, and roads.

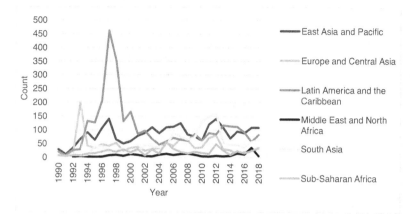

Figure 1.1 Historical Trend of PPI Projects by Region (over the period 1990–2018)

Source: Figure 1.1 was made based on data adapted from World Bank (n.d.). Private participation in infrastructure (PPI) project database. Retrieved June 30, 2019, from https://ppi.worldbank.org/en/ppidata

sector's involvement in energy service areas such as electricity and natural gas has been quite huge and even bigger than that in transport service areas (see Table 1.3). It is also notable that PPI projects have increased in the industry associated with information and communication technology (ICT) over the last two decades.

Another interesting piece of evidence from the database is that the historical trend of PPI projects across regions during the period 1990–2018 has been nonlinear. As shown in Figure 1.1, in the early 1990s, countries in Europe and the Cemtral Asia region were most likely to allow PPI projects in the public sector rather than other countries, but in the mid-1990s, countries in Latin America and the Caribbean region started to introduce PPI projects and in turn they had a peak in the number of projects during 1997. In addition, it is notable that after their recovery from the financial crisis in the late 1990s, mid-income countries (i.e., Hong Kong, South Korea, Taiwan, Malaysia, Singapore, and Indonesia) in East and South Asia have exceeded countries in other regions with respect to the number of PPI projects. This change may be due to the rapid growth in economic development (globalization) in those countries during the 1970s and 1980s and by the so-called top-down national planning and development designed to attract foreign direct investment which in turn helped to bring modern jobs and goods to the region (Common, 2000, pp. 135–136).

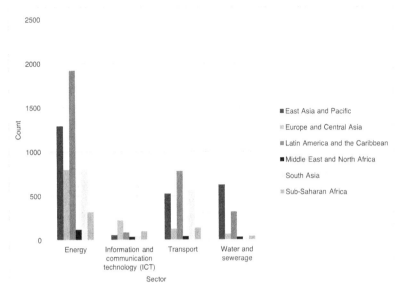

Figure 1.2 PPI Projects by Sector (Disaggregated by Region)

Source: Figure 1.2 was made based on data adapted from World Bank (n.d.). Private participation in infrastructure (PPI) project database. Retrieved June 30, 2019, from https://ppi.worldbank.org/en/ppidata

Furthermore, Figure 1.2 shows the degree to which countries in each region have implemented PPI projects across industry sectors (service areas). It appears that in East Asia countries, PPI projects are largely implemented in the areas of energy and water, and sewerage services. In South Asian countries, the projects have come about to support public energy services as well as transport services. Other countries in the remaining regions, including Europe, Latin America, the Middle East and Africa, seem to have actively allowed the private sector's participation (investment) in projects in the energy sector rather than in other sectors (see Figure 1.2).

3   Definition of PPPs

Despite the widespread attention given to PPPs and their growing popularity in practice around the world, it is interesting to note that there is a lack of an agreed-upon definition of PPPs. According to scholars (e.g., Hodge & Greve, 2005, 2007; Teisman & Klijn, 2002), defining and describing PPPs is indeed a language game. Notions of PPPs still remain multifaceted and inconclusive (Brinkerhoff & Brinkerhoff, 2011; Hodge & Greve, 2007; Smith, Umans, & Thomasson, 2018). Therefore, Hodge (2010) and Hodge and Greve (2013) have pointed out that "[P]PPs can be understood as a specific project or activity, a management tool or organizational form, a policy, a government tool or symbol, or an historical context and a cultural set of assumptions" (Hodge & Greve, 2013, p. 3).

Given this challenge, based on the widely quoted definitions and descriptions of PPPs in the literature, this present study has compartmentalized the PPP concept into three different perspectives at large: (1) institutional, (2) managerial, and (3) relational perspectives. Some representative examples pertaining to each viewpoint found in the public administration and policy literature are as follows:

First, from an institutional perspective, Savas (2000) defines a PPP as "[a]ny arrangement between government and the private sector in which partially or traditionally public activities are performed by the private sector" (p. 4). Similarly, Bovaird (2004) views a PPP as "[w]orking arrangements based on a mutual commitment between a public sector organization and any other organization outside the public sector" (p. 200). Ni (2012) states that "[a] PPP is an institutionalized form of relationship of public and private actors who, in pursuing their respective objectives, work together toward a joint goal" (p. 254). More specifically, Grimsey and Lewis (2007) note that PPPs are "[a]rrangements whereby private parties participate in, or provide support for, the provision of infrastructure" (p. 2). Interestingly, from a somewhat different angle, Hodge and Greve (2007) envision PPPs as "[f]inancial models that enable the public sector to make use of private finance capital in a way that enhances the possibilities of both the elected government and the private company" (p. 546). Indeed, PPPs can be defined as organizational and financial arrangements between two main actors – the public sector and the private counterparts (Hodge & Greve, 2007; Rossi & Civitillo, 2014).

Second, from the managerial perspective, for example, Van Ham and Koppenjan (2001) define a PPP as "[c]ooperation of some sort of durability between public and private actors in which they jointly develop projects and services and share risks, costs, and resources which are connected with these projects" (p. 598). In a similar vein, Koppenjan (2005) describes a PPP as "[a] form of structured cooperation between public and private partners in the planning/construction and/or exploitation of infrastructural facilities in which they share or reallocate risks, costs, benefits, resources, and responsibilities" (p. 137). Marques and Berg (2011) characterize a PPP as "[a] form of public procurement with cooperation between a public authority and a private partner aimed at ensuring the funding, construction, renewal, management and/or maintenance of infrastructure, or the provision of a related service" (p. 1585). Forrer et al. (2010), Engel, Fischer, and Galetovic (2011), and Baker (2016) go further to argue that a PPP is "a long-term contractual arrangement" where the public and private entities can share the design, financing, provision, and management of a public service or an infrastructure project in addition to both the risks and benefits.

Third, from the relational perspective, Rosenau (2000) argues that PPPs refer to public policy networks in which loose stakeholder relationships are emphasized. More specifically, Koppenjan and Klijn (2004) and Steijn, Klijn, and Edelenbos (2011) view that a PPP should be regarded as one type of governance network that has more or less stable patterns of social relations between mutually dependent actors (Steijn et al., 2011, p. 1235). According to Boyer and Newcomer (2015), a PPP is defined as "[a] mutually dependent relationship between the public sector and the private counterpart to construct, renovate and operate a major infrastructure system" (p. 130). Consistent with this viewpoint, Singh and Prakash (2010) and Velotti et al. (2012) point out that a dyadic relationship made up of two organizations in a wider network embodies the nature of PPPs. Further, Brinkerhoff and Brinkerhoff (2011) discuss the broader implications of a PPP (a cross-sectional collaboration), noting it has some critical features, including joint determination of goals, collaborative decision-making, non-hierarchical (horizontal) structures and processes, trust-based and informal relationships, shared accountability for outcomes, and synergistic interactions among partners (p. 4).

From the aforementioned approaches and definitions of a PPP, it can reasonably be concluded that PPPs have been explained in somewhat different ways among scholars. No single dimension (approach) has been able to describe and define the central underlying rationale of PPPs. Given this, it is worthwhile reviewing conceptual emphases and finding some common features embedded in the various definitions of PPPs. Hence, more than 50 scholarly works pertaining to PPPs from recently published articles in public administration and policy-related journals have been examined, and the main (common) components related to PPPs have been set out below (see Table 1.4 and Figure 1.3).

In an attempt to cluster various definitions of PPPs found in the literature and look at stemmed word(s), we used a qualitative software program, NVivo 12. As Table 1.4 and Figure 1.3 display, the absolute and relative frequency (counts) of the word(s) were reported by running "word frequency queries" and exporting "word cloud visualizations." It was found that 'public,' 'private,' 'long(term),' 'sector,' 'services,' 'partnership(s),' 'infrastructure,' 'government,' 'risks,' 'actors,' and 'project' are among the most frequently referenced word groups.

Table 1.4 Word Frequency Query Results (Selective ones)

Word	Count	Word	Count
Public	58	Private	49
Long (term)	22	Sector	20
Services	15	Partnership(s)	14
Infrastructure	14	Government	13
Risks	13	Actors	12
Project	10	Organizations	9
Provision	8	Costs	8
Partnerships	7	Contractual	7
Joint	6	Financing	6
Contract	4	Shared	6
Responsibilities	4	Cooperation	4
Collaboration/ Collaborative	3	Resources	4
Hybrid	3	Contracting	3

Source: Author's own calculations

Figure 1.3 Word Cloud Output of Public-Private Partnerships (PPPs)

Source: Author's own elaboration

Overall, it can be acknowledged that PPPs tend to be defined in the following aspects in a broader manner: (1) public- and private-sector (actors), (2) long-term impacts, (3) infrastructure projects (government services), (4) service provisions, (5) shared risks and responsibilities, (6) contractual relationships, (7) collaborations, (8) cooperation, (9) joint/hybrid works, (10) costs/financing, and so on. They seem to be in line with previous studies (e.g., Gunawansa, 2010; Hodge & Greve, 2005, 2007; Klijn & Teisman, 2003; Savas, 2000; Warsen, Nederhand, Klijn, Grotenbreg, & Koppenjan, 2018) emphasizing the significance of long-term partnering relationships, risk-sharing, joint decision-making (projection), and cooperation between public and private entities.

4 Types of PPPs

Similar to the definitions of PPPs, no single type (form) of PPPs can explain the entire set of PPPs. From a macro-level perspective, PPPs have been implemented and managed somewhat differently depending on the service areas (industries), market contexts, and institutional settings (e.g., legal and political institutions) in many countries around the world. For instance, focusing on the purpose of PPPs, Brinkerhoff and Brinkerhoff (2011, p. 8) argue that there are five major types of PPPs at large, noting that each PPP type has diverse organizational structures and related processes as follows: (1) Policy PPPs (Network, Task force, Joint committee, and Special commission), (2) Service delivery PPPs (Co-production, Joint venture, Contract, and Partnership agreement, also known as MOU), (3) Infrastructure PPPs (Joint venture, Build-operate-transfer, Build-operate-own-transfer, and Design-build-operate), (4) Capacity-building PPPs (Knowledge network, Twinning, Contract, and Partnership agreement), (5) Economic development PPPs (Joint venture, Contract, Partnership agreement).

From a micro-level viewpoint, in practice, types of PPPs appear to vary depending on the degree of private involvement in each stage of PPP projects – largely ranging from design, build, finance, ownership, and operation, to transfer (Hodge & Greve, 2007). Scholars in the area of public administration and policy have named the types of PPPs in very different ways. Acknowledging this, this section narrows the focus to introduce some of the most widely cited PPP types in past and recent scholarship.

First, Hodge and Greve (2007) noted a three-way classification regarding infrastructure projects: (1) BOT (Build-Own-Transfer), (2) BOOT (Build-Own-Operate-Transfer), and (3) sale-and-lease-back arrangements. The first and second types of PPPs commonly represent that a private partner (firm) should be in charge of building a facility (building) at its own expense and then sometimes operating that facility, and upon completion of the project (or at the time the concession period ends), transferring the property rights to the government agencies. But it should be noted that the second type of PPP requires the private firm to retain the right to operate the facility because the firm uses its own funds to proceed with the project. The third type of PPP occurs, for example, when governments sell their buildings and then rent them back later from a financial organization via a contract over a period of about 20 to 30 years (Hodge & Greve, 2007, p. 546).

Similarly, Silvestre and Araújo (2012, pp. 321–322) viewed recently implemented PPP contracts in one or another of the following four different forms: (1) Lease-Build-Operate (LBO), (2) Build-Transfer-Operate (BTO), (3) Built-Own-Operate-Transfer (BOOT), and (4) Buy-Build-Operate (BBO). The first form of PPP represents one where the private partner should be responsible for building and operating certain public services (or a facility) but needs to pay a fee to the government. The related long-term return on investment (ROI) is revenue derived from user fees. The second type of PPP occurs when, after building and delivering the public services, the private partner needs to transfer property rights to the public sector but may continue to run the services under a contract. For this, user fees are also collected as revenue. The third kind of PPP is the same as the BOOT type in Hodge and Greve's (2007) classification. In other words, the private partner can continue to operate the related services and collect user fees to recover the ROI by themselves. The last type is different from the aforementioned kinds of PPPs. In this case, the private organizations initially purchase property rights for the government-owned facility or public services from government agencies and then develop and operate them in the long term. Interestingly, sometimes a franchise payment to the government will be expected.

More specifically, other scholars (e.g., see Perez & March, 2006; Ni, 2012) have categorized the means by which public services are designated and delivered (project delivery options *per se*) through PPPs into the following six approaches: (1) Design-Build (DB), (2) Design-Build-Operate (DBO), Design-Build-Maintain (DBM), and Design-Build-Operate-Maintain (DBOM), (3) Design-Build-Operate-Turnover (DBOT), Build-Operate-Transfer (BOT), and Design-Build-Warranty (DBW), (4) Build-Own-Operate (BOO), Buy-Build-Operate (BBO), and Buy/Lease-Develop-Operate (BDO), (5) Maintenance and Operation, and (6) Program Management and Strategic Planning (Ni, 2012, pp. 255–256).

Although research has documented apparent categorical differences and private-sector service-delivery foci among the different types of PPPs, for typical (traditional) types of PPP projects, there has been a commonly held perception that private partner(s) are able to participate in designing, building and/or operating (maintaining) a facility in accordance with the contract agreement within an agreed-upon time frame and at a predetermined price. In addition, once completed, the private counterparts can transfer the facility to government agencies. In this case, they tend to provide a warranty to guarantee the facility's condition. If necessary, they also should be engaged in renovating, modernizing, and expanding the facility. And then the private partners may operate it under a contract with government agencies. Of course, government agencies are able to simply outsource the maintenance and operation of the facility to private companies. Further, the private partners are expected to support government projects (mostly large, complex projects), improve program management, or develop strategic planning associated with the design, construction, and activities of a facility.

5 Determinants of PPPs

Why do some governments adopt PPPs while others do not? Generally speaking, it can be reasonably argued that PPPs have been adopted because governments need to meet growing public needs (demands) more effectively by using the private sector's expertise, information, and capital (resources) (MOF, 2012). In the words of Forrer et al. (2010),

> [I]n a globalizing world that is more integrated, complex and volatile, governments simply may not possess the prerequisite knowledge, capacity or managerial skills . . . governments need to engage partners that have the necessary expertise, know-how, and managerial adeptness needed to carry out government responsibilities.
>
> (p. 477)

In recent years, governments' willingness to adopt PPPs is likely to be more conditional and strategic and appears to be intertwined with a government's desire for smoothing the effect of widespread fiscal stress and achieving improved public performance, cost reduction (cost savings), higher levels of competition in the global market, or environmental protection (Miller, 2000; Ni, 2012). Therefore, to answer the aforementioned basic policy adoption question more specifically, there is a need to closely look at the set of motivating factors (determinants) of PPPs within the developed/developing economy dichotomy (developed versus developing countries), such as socio-economic and demographic conditions and their historical changes, political environment/ideology, election cycles (years), legal institutions, interest groups, societal and cultural expectations, and previous PPP experience in each country (e.g., for more information, see Hammami, Ruhashyankiko, & Yehoue, 2006; Hyun, Park, & Tian, 2018; Wang & Zhao, 2014).

As discussed earlier in this chapter, some European countries (i.e., UK and France) had struggled with a lack of (public) funding sources to support their infrastructure projects, which can help lead to enhanced community development and economic growth in the long term (Hodge & Greve, 2007; Osborne, 2001). This appears to be the main reason why PPPs have been initially implemented in developed countries. Moreover, the need for sharing and allocating risks among all stakeholders associated with a project was another key reason for developed countries to lower the burden of risk-averse public actors (Gunawansa, 2010, p. 442). For developing countries with transitional economies, Gunawansa (2010) argues that the need for sufficient financial resources, modern technology, and efficient management skills for economic development have been considered as the main determinants of PPP operations (p. 442).

Beyond such generally accepted rationales, recent empirical research has provided evidence indicating that PPPs in developing countries are likely to be affected by diverse internal and external factors. For example, during 1990–2003, Hammami et al. (2006) explored determinants of PPPs for infrastructure in developing countries based on the World Bank's Private Participation in Infrastructure (PPI) database. They basically posited that the PPP drivers vary across service areas (industries) and depend on the nature of public infrastructure. In their study, it was found that "[P]PPs are more likely to be common in countries where governments suffer from heavy debt burdens and where market size is large enough to allow for cost recovery" (Hammami et al., 2006, p. 4). Their findings also revealed that countries with less corruption, experience with PPP operations, and effective rule of law are more likely to adopt PPPs rather than countries where this is not the case.

Drawing upon Berry and Berry's (1990) widely cited policy adoption/diffusion framework – internal determinants versus external (neighboring) influences,[2] Wang and Zhao (2014) investigated the case of Toll Road Financing through PPPs. Based on US data during the period 1985–2010, they empirically examined which factors (determinants) have been highly influential in the adoption of PPPs for highway tolling projects in state governments. In terms of internal determinants of PPPs, citizens' demands (e.g., traffic control), fiscal pressures, state wealth (e.g., a higher state income level), PPP legislation, and the number of PPP projects in the state (earlier experiences of PPPs) turned out to have a significant and positive influence on the adoption of PPPs. On the other hand, liberal political ideology and public employees' resistance to change turned out to be negatively associated with the adoption of PPPs. With respect to external influences, somewhat unexpectedly the number of neighboring states that have adopted PPPs appeared to have a negative impact on PPP adoption. This implies that governments indeed learn from each other because the effects of seeing unsuccessful PPP cases may certainly work as a strong barrier to a state's willingness to adopt PPPs.

Focusing on PPP investments in infrastructure in developing countries (mostly in Asia), Hyun et al. (2018) found that macro-economic factors such as the degree of economic growth or inflation are the most relevant determinants of PPP projects. Consistent with Hammami et al.'s (2006) and Wang and Zhao's (2014) findings, it was also found that the least corrupt (or corrupt-free) countries and those with previous PPP experience are more willing to implement innovative project operations through PPPs than others.

6 The PPP debate: advantages and disadvantages

It should not be surprising that some scholars and practitioners are more likely to prefer adopting and implementing PPPs for civil infrastructure, while others tend to be more critical of them. Notably, the argument in favor of PPPs and the counterarguments should be viewed as providing only suggestive rather than conclusive evidence because the impact of PPPs on each state or society still remains an ongoing topic of debate.

Despite mixed and inconclusive arguments and evidence, first of all, one can argue that "better value for money (VFM)" has long been held as one of the primary advantages of a typical PPP project in the literature and government documents (e.g., Hodge & Greve, 2007; Hwang, Zhao, & Gay, 2013; MOF, 2012; Smith et al., 2018; Warsen et al., 2018). In PPP projects, by switching the role of government from a service provider to a service purchaser, public agencies are expected to keep utilizing private-sector resources (mostly finance capital) and experience much lower levels of financial burden in delivering goods and services over the project's whole life cycle (Savas, 2000; Smith et al., 2018). Thus, as Hodge and Greve (2007) argue, because pressure on government budgets is reduced, PPPs allow governments to have a greater capacity to spend on other policy priorities (p. 548).

Second, PPPs enable the public sector not only to enjoy financial and material benefits (e.g., profits and increased transport capacity) through private partner engagement in the projects (Klijn & Teisman, 2003) but also to have access to the intangible, special expertise (knowledge) and management know-how of the private sector, including better technology, enhanced commercial potential of the project, competitiveness, and innovative solutions for the desired public service delivery (Brinkerhoff & Brinkerhoff, 2011; Forrer et al., 2010; MOF, 2012). In doing so, it can be reasonably expected that PPPs provide better performance (improved service quality or diversity) compared to more traditionally tendered projects (Ewoh & Zimerman, 2010; Hodge & Greve, 2005; Savas, 2000; Warsen et al., 2018).

Third, while allocating or sharing risks embedded into PPP projects to either side (according to each party's expertise), stakeholders in the public and private sectors are more likely to focus on the ways of seeking desired service production and delivery together (Hodge & Greve, 2007; MOF, 2012). For example, as in the Public Private Partnership Handbook of Singapore (MOF, 2012), while government agencies can take on political and regulatory risks, business firms can deal with risks pertaining to design, construction, and financing in a broader manner. In pursuit of common (mutual) goals, government and private firms can work together as partners in the long term. For this, in practice, a few critical conditions may be required, such as a commitment between two or more parties engaged in a PPP project, consistent communication between government and private partners, well-defined responsibilities and authority, trust-based relationships, and consensus-based decision-making (e.g., see Brinkerhoff & Brinkerhoff, 2011; Zhang, 2005).

Lastly, PPPs can offer a so-called win-win solution to all stakeholders in the public sector, the private sector, and with the public (people sector) (MOF, 2012, pp. 6–7). Specifically speaking, through PPPs, the public sector can basically benefit from the private firms' cost-efficient (cost-saving) operation of services within the given timeframe (Savas, 2000; Yang, Hou, & Wang, 2013). Besides, the private sector can also benefit from government support toward more business opportunities and by introducing new services or innovation into the financing and management of government assets and services (Marques & Berg, 2011). With the support from the public sector, the private counterparts can gain various tax incentives, stable cash flow, and further reasonable returns on their investments (profit generation through recurrent income streams over a certain period of time) (e.g., for more information, see Hwang et al., 2013; Kouwenhoven, 1993; Ni, 2012; Ping & Trager, 2014; Yang et al., 2013). Furthermore, PPPs can ensure greater benefits to the public eventually in that civil infrastructure is a way to meet public policy goals and needs (Li, Akintoye, Edwards, & Hardcastle, 2005).

On the other side of the coin, there are, of course, several noted disadvantages of PPPs. First, without proper legal safeguards and strong (and specific) managerial guidelines, PPPs will easily fail to provide a satisfactory level of service performance. Although the PPP stakeholders are expected to be more accountable to the government and customers (citizens) due to the presence of rewards and penalties in the contract (Marques & Berg, 2011), the greater the scale of PPP projects, the greater the likelihood of being exposed to mismanagement and corruption (Coghill & Woodward, 2005; Landow & Ebdon, 2012). From this perspective, some scholars (e.g., see Bloomfield, Westerling, & Carey, 1998; Greve, 2003; Hodge & Greve,

2007; Marques & Berg, 2011; Warsen et al., 2018) point out that compared to traditional procurement (e.g., public works or outsourcing contracts), PPPs in infrastructure projects have been more associated with time delays, financial risks, and scandals such as fraud, waste (cost overrun), abuse, and false accounting (disguising the real costs), thereby leading to more debt for governments or higher taxes for citizens. Presumably, this is attributable to uncertainty within PPPs and the complexity in their nature (largely due to a longer period of time), the inexperience of the public and private sectors (unfamiliarity with the PPP mechanism), or the reluctance to share risks with counterparts (Gunawansa, 2010; Landow & Ebdon, 2012; Li et al., 2005; Savas, 2000; Van Slyke, 2009).

Second, because the goals of the public sector and the private partners basically diverge, many PPPs may face agency problems that stem from conflicts of interest, self-interested contractor's opportunistic behaviors, or asymmetric information (Edwards & Shaoul, 2003; Savas, 2000; Sclar, 2000; Smith et al., 2018; Van Slyke, 2009). In turn, there is no guarantee that performance expectations can always be met and the public interest can be protected. In this vein, Smith et al. (2018, p. 101) argue that "[a]gency problems are most likely to occur during the effort to achieve mutuality, because partners in PPPs come from different sectors and possess unequal power in the partnership."

In addition, there has been concern over how to measure the service performance of PPPs. While acknowledging that further research into performance evaluation of PPPs is needed, scholars have pointed out the difficulty of identifying clear and relevant performance indicators across diverse PPP projects (Baker, 2016; Smith et al., 2018; Yang et al., 2013). Nonetheless, it can be reasonably expected that performance measures may include the quality of service provided, cost-effectiveness (actual service cost in comparison with expected one), and other public values such as transparency, equity, and accountability.

7 A review: theoretical approaches to PPPs

Initial scholarly attention regarding the positive influence of private involvement in public management can be traced to traditional public choice theory. From this theoretical perspective, public organizations and employees tend to become incompetent or inefficient in providing public goods and services, particularly in managing (reducing) costs. This is attributable to "*typically highly bureaucratic*" organizational structures embedded in the public sector (Hammami et al., 2006, p. 5). These characteristics of public bureaus lead public management systems to become monopolistic and inflexible in their practice. Acknowledging these challenges, scholars have long argued that externalizing service production (market-oriented provision) rather than keeping it under the influence of the bureaucracy (in-house [direct] provision) is likely to ensure the delivery of better services at a lower cost, a retention of flexibility and competition in the process, the utilization of specialized technical skills, funding, knowledge, or know-how offered by the private sector, and also the ability to offer greater customer choice (e.g., see Ferris, 1986; Forrer et al., 2010; Hefetz & Warner, 2012; Kettl, 1993; Osborne, 2001; Savas, 2000). In this vein, Hammami et al. (2006) emphasize the significance of PPPs in that by involving private partners in government program delivery, inefficient public spending is reduced and instead public organizations are allowed to respond to market forces and innovation to overcome the lack of their managerial skills in the area of complex infrastructure projects.

In line with the abovementioned generic viewpoint, to date, a large body of literature on PPPs has further relied on two generally accepted theoretical approaches – principal-agent theory and transaction cost theory – to frame their analyses. These theories provide several rationales as to why PPPs can resolve a situation in which governments find it challenging to manage PPP projects effectively and how policymakers can tackle a propensity of mismanagement and corruption problems. First of all, the principal-agent theory implicitly assumes that in a PPP context, there are two rational, self-interested actors – the principal and agent: the principal represents a public authority, whereas the agent represents its private counterparts (here, investors or developers, called contractors) (Smith et al., 2018). As discussed earlier in this chapter, in long-term ongoing partnering relationships, both principals and agents are expected to commonly take up leading roles in making decisions and sharing risks.

Specifically, however, during the contract period, while the public partner (principal) is highly charged with oversight responsibility and has control over the quantity and quality of the services delivered to users, the private partner (agent) is obligated to be held accountable for making the best investment choices and optimizing costs during the construction and operation phases, respectively (Baker, 2016, p. 434; Iossa & Martimort, 2015). Besides, the public partner as a principal tends to play a leading role as a regulator as well as an arbitrator, sometimes in cases where regulatory bodies and the courts are subject to government influences (Baker, 2016, p. 432). In such a situation there is also an unequal power distribution between these two actors in the transaction-based contract. They basically have different orientations/motives (welfare maximization versus profit maximization)[3] and subsequent conflicting interests, and, in turn, they (mostly principals) are likely to struggle with the challenges associated with asymmetric information (e.g., adverse selection and moral hazard) and uncertainty (e.g., the risk of opportunism) over the period of long-term contractual relationships (Eisenhardt, 1989; Smith et al., 2018; Soomro & Zhang, 2015). Such agency problems appear to jeopardize the efficacy of PPP projects in the short run and hinder the expansion of PPP markets in the long run (Baker, 2016, p. 451).

Second, some of the leading scholars supporting transaction-cost theory (e.g., Coase, 1937; Simon, 1972; Williamson, 1975, 1981) have long viewed that transaction-based contracts are not necessarily complete due to the bounded rationality of human agents and their opportunistic (shirking) behaviors, leading to extra costs and burdens being placed on governments (principals). Kim (2017) agrees with this point, stating that "[c]ontractors have better information about their day-to-day service delivery operations and more professional expertise than governments do, and information about their behaviors are not easily observed by the principal . . . therefore, [it] may cause inefficiency and unavoidable high transaction costs" (p. 757). Brown and Potoski (2005) provide a deeper discussion about these costs, focusing on two service-specific factors initially identified by Williamson (1981): ease of measurement and asset specificity (p. 329). They argue that "[t]he costs of negotiating, implementing, monitoring, and enforcing contracts are higher when services have outcomes that are difficult to measure and when services require asset-specific investments that increase the likelihood of monopoly markets" (Brown & Potoski, 2005, p. 327). Furthermore, beyond the typical transaction (management) costs associated with the government's screening (the so-called tendering phase of PPP deals), preparing contracts, negotiating, supervision, or monitoring works, other scholars (e.g., see Baker, 2016; Soliño & de Santos, 2016) maintain a closer look at additional 'ex-ante' and 'ex-post' costs (including hidden costs) and find that they mostly stem from the partners' opportunistic behaviors motivated by self-interest,[4] complexity of the PPP project, and unforeseen events that may happen during the contract period of PPPs. When considered together, it seems evident that in cases where transaction costs indeed outweigh potential benefits of PPPs, government agencies will eventually struggle with PPP failure.

In the wake of potential risks of the PPP management process, Baker (2016) insists that the size and scope of such costs can be minimized depending on how well property is protected and rules are defined and enforced (p. 438). In short, a state's institutional (regulatory) quality such as property and contractual rights, especially in developing countries, matters for the success of PPP projects. On the other hand, to ensure that highly risk-averse agents' behaviors in pursuit of their own self-interest become aligned with those of the principals, and also to lower transaction costs embedded in PPPs, Soliño and de Santos (2016) point out the necessity of incentives (control mechanisms *per se*) in the tendering, contract-awarding, and operating phases of PPPs. Examples of incentives can be market competition, asset ownership, risk sharing, or enhanced reputation (Soliño & de Santos, 2016, p. 100). Likewise, Warsen, Klijn, and Koppenjan (2019) argue that to ensure the agents perform well and abide by the contract, the role of payments, sanctions, and performance indicators of PPPs is indeed important. In a broader array of government contracting, Kim (2017, 2019) envisions that monitoring-based incentives and penalties can help deter the opportunism of self-interested agents and further decrease transaction costs. While positive incentives (rewards) for satisfactory performance of private partners may include, for example, the granting of contract extensions and renewals, giving constant feedback and/or discretion, and financial inducements (e.g., bonus payments), negative incentives (sanctions) for poor or unsatisfactory performance of private counterparts may involve monetary penalties, contract termination, prohibition from future tendering/procurement practices and legal litigation (Brown & Potoski, 2005; Girth, 2012; Kim, 2015, 2019).

In addition, it is notable that the focus of recent PPP literature has been to uncover why relational factors (conditions) rather than transactional factors matter for the growth and success of PPPs. Now that participating actors (partners) in PPP projects tend to continue to be dependent on each other during the long-term contract period and one (perhaps the private partner) might possess more resources than the other (the government agency) (Klijn & Teisman, 2003) point out that the public-sector actors will need to strategically manage ongoing partnering relationships to hold their counterparts accountable for their decisions and subsequent performance. With the view that private-sector actors play a role as more pro-organizational partners (stewards *per se*) than self-interested agents in a government contract setting including PPPs, this theoretical stream seems to provide useful insights to supplement the generally accepted theories discussed above, including the principal-agent theory and transaction cost theory, and suggests a well-rounded, ideal partnership relationship (Kim, 2015, 2017, p. 758). In the words of Amirkhanyan, Kim, and Lambright (2012),

> [T]ransaction contracts are short-term, economic exchanges based on carefully detailed contractual agreements and close oversight of the provider's compliance. In contrast, relational contracts are based on open-ended long-term exchanges in which personal ties and informal communication foster trust and flexible approaches to solving implementation problems.
>
> (p. 344)

Consistent with this viewpoint, public administration scholars have highlighted the role of collaborative (network-based) management, cooperation and trust-building between the partners, and informational communication and openness in PPPs (e.g., see Klijn & Teisman, 2003; Van Slyke, 2009; Warsen et al., 2019). These are believed to help government agencies and managers to be less vulnerable to the opportunism of self-interested agents in the short term and to reduce transaction costs and ensure accountability in the entire PPP process in the long term. Interestingly, according to Sclar (2000), Brown, Potoski, and Van Slyke (2006), and Amirkhanyan, Kim, and Lambright (2010), relational contracts tend to be used in situations in which government contracting faces high-level asset specificity and uncertainty (Kim, 2015).

Notes

1 The time span of PPPs varies across governments or areas. PPPs often tend to extend beyond 30–40 years (Boyer & Newcomer, 2015). For example, in the United Kingdom, PPPs tend to last for 30 years in general, whereas in the United States, some PPPs have operated for over a century (Forrer et al., 2010, p. 478).
2 Neighboring influences refer to neighboring governments (other states or countries) that already experienced PPP activities (a policy diffusion factor *per se*).
3 There is a general understanding that both principals and agents are considered as utility maximizers (social utility versus personal/private utility) with bounded rationality (Kim, 2015, 2017; Soliño & de Santos, 2016; Williamson, 1981).
4 The related costs, for example, include renegotiation costs and costs arising from litigation among partners (Soliño & de Santos, 2016, pp. 112–113).

References

Amirkhanyan, A. A., Kim, H. J., & Lambright, K. T. (2010). Do relationships matter? Assessing the association between relationship design and contractor performance. *Public Performance & Management Review, 34*(2), 189–220.

Amirkhanyan, A. A., Kim, H. J., & Lambright, K. T. (2012). Closer than "arms length": Understanding the factors associated with collaborative contracting. *American Review of Public Administration, 42*(3), 341–366.

Baker, N. B. (2016). Transaction costs in public-private partnerships: The weight of institutional quality in developing countries revisited. *Public Performance & Management Review, 40*(2), 431–455.

Berry, F. S., & Berry, W. D. (1990). State lottery adoptions as policy innovations: An event history analysis. *American Political Science Review, 84*(2), 396–415.

Bloomfield, P., Westerling, D., & Carey, R. (1998). Innovation and risks in a public-private partnership: Financing and construction of a capital project in Massachusetts. *Public Productivity and Management Review, 21*(4), 460–471.

Bovaird, T. (2004). Public-private partnerships in Western Europe and the US: New growths from old roots. In A. Ghobadian, D. Gallear, N. O'Regan, & H. Viney

(Eds.), *Public-private partnerships: Policy and experience* (pp. 221–250). London, UK: Palgrave Macmillan.

Boyer, E. J., & Newcomer, K. E. (2015). Developing government expertise in strategic contracting for public-private partnerships. *Journal of Strategic Contracting and Negotiation, 1*(2), 129–148.

Brinkerhoff, D. W., & Brinkerhoff, J. M. (2011). Public-private partnerships: Perspectives on purposes, publicness, and good governance. *Public Administration and Development, 31*(1), 2–14.

Brown, T. L. & Potoski, M. (2005). Transaction costs and contracting: The practitioner perspective. *Public Performance & Management Review, 28*(3), 326–351.

Brown, T. L., Potoski, M., & Van Slyke, D. M. (2006). Managing public service contracts: Aligning values, institutions, and markets. *Public Administration Review, 66*(3), 323–332.

Coase, R. H. (1937). The nature of the firm. *Economica, 4*(16), 386–405.

Coghill, K., & Woodward, D. (2005). Political issues of public-private partnerships. In G. Hodge & C. Greve (Eds.), *The challenge of public-private partnerships: Learning from international experience* (pp. 81–94). Cheltenham, UK: Edward Elgar.

Common, R. (2000). The East Asia region: Do public-private partnerships make sense? In S. P. Osborne (Ed.), *Public-private partnerships: Theory and practice in international perspective* (pp. 134–148). New York, NY: Routledge.

Corner, D. (2005). The United Kingdom private finance initiative: The challenge of allocating risk. In G. Hodge & C. Greve (Eds.), *The challenge of public-private partnerships: Learning from international experience* (pp. 44–61). Cheltenham, UK: Edward Elgar.

Edwards, P., & Shaoul, J. (2003). Partnerships: For better, for worse? *Accounting, Auditing and Accountability Journal, 16*(3), 397–421.

Eisenhardt, K. M. (1989). Agency theory: An assessment and review. *The Academy of Management Review, 14*(1), 57–74.

Engel, E. M., Fischer, R. D., & Galetovic, A. (2011). The basic public finance of public-private partnerships. *Cowles Foundation Discussion Paper No. 1618; Yale University Economic Growth Center Discussion Paper No. 957; Yale Economics Department Working Paper No. 35*. Retrieved from SSRN: https://ssrn.com/abstract=1001212

European Investment Bank. (2017). Total value of European PPP projects by sector – all countries and Number of European PPP projects by sector – all countries. *European PPP Expertise Centre (EPEC) Data Portal*. Retrieved August 12, 2019, from https://data.eib.org/epec

Evans, J., & Bowman, D. (2005). Getting the contract right. In G. Hodge & C. Greve (Eds.), *The challenge of public-private partnerships* (pp. 62–80). Cheltenham, UK: Edward Elgar.

Ewoh, A. I. E., & Zimerman, U. (2010). Public-private collaborations: The case of Atlanta Metro Community Improvement District Alliance. *Public Performance & Management Review, 33*(3), 395–412.

Ferris, J. M. (1986). The decision to contract out: An empirical analysis. *Urban Affairs Quarterly, 22*(2), 289–311.

Forrer, J., Kee, J. E., Newcomer, K. E., & Boyer, E. (2010). Public-private partnerships and the public accountability question. *Public Administration Review*, *70*(3), 475–484.

Girth, A. M. (2012). A closer look at contract accountability: Exploring the determinants of sanctions of unsatisfactory contract performance. *Journal of Public Administration Research and Theory*, *23*(3), 1–32.

Greve, C., & Ejersbo, N. (2003, September 3). When public-private partnerships fail: The extreme case of the NPM-inspired local government of Farum in Denmark. *Paper presented at the European Group of Public Administration Conference*. Oerias, Portugal.

Grimsey, D., & Lewis, M. (2007). Public private partnerships and public procurement. *Agenda: A Journal of Policy Analysis and Reform*, *14*(2), 171–188.

Gunawansa, A. (2010). Is there a need for public private partnership projects in Singapore? *COBRA 2010 – Construction, Building and Real Estate Research Conference of the Royal Institution of Chartered Surveyors*. Singapore: Scholar-Bank@NUS Repository. Retrieved June 28, 2019, from https://scholarbank.nus.edu.sg/handle/10635/45950

Hammami, M., Ruhashyankiko, J.-F., & Yehoue, E. B. (2006). Determinants of public-private partnerships in infrastructure. *IMF Working Paper No. 06/99*. IMF. Retrieved July 30, 2019, from www.imf.org/external/pubs/ft/wp/2006/wp0699.pdf

Hefetz, A., & Warner, M. (2012). Contracting or public delivery? The importance of service, market and management characteristics. *Journal of Public Administration Research and Theory*, *22*(2), 289–317.

Hodge, G. (2010, November). On evaluating PPP success: Thoughts for our future. *Key note address to the Finnish Association of Administrative Sciences*. Helsinki, Finland.

Hodge, G., & Greve, C. (2005). *The challenge of public-private partnerships: Learning from international experience*. Cheltenham, UK: Edward Elgar.

Hodge, G., & Greve, C. (2007). Public-private partnerships: An international performance review. *Public Administration Review*, *67*(3), 545–558.

Hodge, G., & Greve, C. (2013). Introduction. In Public-private partnership in turbulent times. In C. Greve & G. Hodge (Eds.), *Rethinking public-private partnerships: Strategies for turbulent times* (pp. 1–32). Abingdon, UK: Routledge.

Hwang, B., Zhao, X., & Gay, M. (2013). Public private partnership projects in Singapore: Factors, critical risks and preferred risk allocation from the perspective of contractors. *International Journal of Project Management*, *31*(3), 424–433.

Hyun, S., Park, D., & Tian, S. (2018). *Determinants of public-private partnerships in infrastructure in Asia: Implications for capital market development*. Asian Development Bank (ADB) Economics Working Paper Series. No. 552. Retrieved October 29, 2019, from https://www.adb.org/sites/default/files/publication/438966/ewp-552-ppps-infrastructure-asia-capital-market.pdf

Iossa, E., & Martimort, D. (2015). The simple micro-economics of public-private partnerships. *Journal of Public Economic Theory*, *17*(1), 4–48.

Kettl, D. F. (1988). *Government by proxy – (Mis?) managing federal programs*. Washington, DC: The Congressional Quarterly Press.

Kettl, D. F. (1993). *Sharing power: Public governance and private markets*. Washington, DC: The Brookings Institution.

Kim, S. (2015). *Toward financially effective contract management: Comparing perceptions of contract managers in the public and private sectors* (Doctoral dissertation, Rutgers, The State University of New Jersey). Retrieved from https://rucore.libraries.rutgers.edu/rutgers-lib/47684/PDF/1/play/

Kim, S. (2017). Lessons learned from public and private contract managers for effective local government contracting out: The case of New Jersey. *International Journal of Public Administration, 40*(9), 756–769.

Kim, S. (2019). Understanding and operationalizing financial accountability in government contracting systems. In A. Farazmand (Ed.), *Global encyclopedia of public administration, public policy, and governance*. Cham: Springer.

Klijn, E. H., & Teisman, G. R. (2003). Institutional and strategic barriers to public-private partnership: An analysis of Dutch cases. *Public Money & Management, 23*(3), 137–146.

Koppell, J. G. S. (2003). *The politics of quasi-government: Hybrid organizations and the dynamics of bureaucratic control*. New York, NY: Cambridge University Press.

Koppenjan J. F. M. (2005). The formation of public-private partnerships: Lessons from nine transport infrastructure projects in the Netherlands. *Public Administration, 83*(1), 135–157.

Koppenjan, J. F. M., & Klijn, E. H. (2004). *Managing uncertainties in networks: A network approach to problem solving and decision making*. London, UK: Routledge.

Kouwenhoven, V. (1993). Public-private partnership: A model for the management of public-private cooperation. In J. Kooiman (Ed.), *Modern governance: New government-society interactions* (pp. 119–130). London, UK: Sage.

Kumaraswamy, M. M., & Morris, D. A. (2002). Build-operate-transfer-type procurement in Asian megaprojects. *Journal of Construction Engineering and Management, 128*(2), 93–102.

Lam, P. (2004). Public private partnerships and the search for value. *Ethos, 10*(2), 9–12. Retrieved June 26, 2019, from https://wpqr4.adb.org/LotusQuickr/copmfdr/PageLibrary482571AE005630C2.nsf/0/7B0B13BED18524A648257C3C0019CA11/$file/Day%202_Singapore%20_PPP%20Ethos%20article_WTan.pdf

Landow, P., & Ebdon, C. (2012). Public-private partnerships, public authorities, and democratic governance. *Public Performance & Management Review, 35*(4), 727–752.

Leigland, J. (2018). Public-private partnerships in developing countries: The emerging evidence-based critique. *The World Bank Research Observer, 33*(1), 103–134.

Li, B., Akintoye, A., Edwards, P. J., & Hardcastle, C. (2005). Critical success factors for PPP/PFI projects in the UK construction industry. *Construction Management and Economics, 23*(5), 459–471.

Marques, R. C., & Berg, S. (2011). Public-private partnership contracts: A tale of two cities with different contractual arrangements. *Public Administration, 89*(4), 1585–1603.

Miller, J. B. (2000). *Principles of public and private infrastructure delivery*. Boston, MA: Kluwer Academic Publishers.

Milward, H. B., & Provan, K. G. (2000). Governing the hollow state. *Journal of Public Administration Research and Theory, 10*(2), 359–380.

Ministry of Finance (MOF), Singapore. (2012). *Public private partnership handbook: Version 2.* Retrieved June 25, 2019, from www.mof.gov.sg/Portals/0/Policies/ProcurementProcess/PPPHandbook2012.pdf

Ni, A. Y. (2012). The risk-averting game of transport public-private partnership: Lessons from the adventure of California's state route 91 express lanes. *Public Performance & Management Review, 36*(2), 253–274.

Osborne, S. (2001). *Public-private partnerships: Theory and practice in international perspective.* New York, NY: Routledge.

Peters, B. G. (1998). With a little help from our friends: Public-private partnerships as institutions and instruments. In J. Pierre (Ed.), *Partnerships in urban governance* (pp. 1–10). New York, NY: St. Martin's Press.

Perez, B. G., & March, J. W. (2006). *Public-private partnerships and the development of transport infrastructure: Trends on both sides of the Atlantic.* Alberta, Canada: University of Alberta, Institute of Public Economics.

Ping, T. J., & Trager, A. M. (2014). Making public-private partnerships work: Implications for Singapore and the region. *Ethos, 13*, 96–102. Retrieved June 27, 2019, from www.sais-jhu.edu/sites/default/files/ThiaJP%26ATrager%20final.pdf

Rosenau, V. P. (2000). *Public-private policy partnerships.* Cambridge, MA: MIT Press.

Rossi, M., & Civitillo, R. (2014). Public private partnerships: A general overview in Italy. *Procedia – Social and Behavioral Sciences, 109*, 140–149.

Salamon, L. M. (1981). Rethinking public management: Third-party government and the changing forms of government action. *Public Policy, 29*(3), 255–275.

Savas, E. S. (2000). *Privatization and public-private partnerships.* New York, NY: Chatham House.

Sclar, E. D. (2000). *You don't always get what you pay for: The economics of privatization.* Ithaca, NY: Cornell University Press.

Silvestre, H. C., & de Araújo, J. F. F. E. (2012). Public-private partnerships/private finance initiatives in Portugal: Theory, practice, and results. *Public Performance & Management Review, 36*(2), 316–339.

Simon, H. (1972). Theories of bounded rationality. In C. B. McGuire & R. Radner (Eds.), *Decision and organization* (pp. 161–176). Amsterdam: North-Holland.

Singh, A., & Prakash, G. (2010). Public-private partnerships in health services delivery: A network organizations perspective. *Public Management Review, 12*(6), 829–856.

Smith, E., Umans, T., & Thomasson, A. (2018). Stages of PPP and principal-agent conflicts: The Swedish water and sewerage sector. *Public Performance & Management Review, 41*(1), 100–129.

Smith, S. R., & Lipsky, M. (1993). *Non-profits for hire: The welfare state in the age of contracting.* Cambridge, MA: Harvard University Press.

Soliño, A. S., & de Santos, P. G. (2016). Influence of the tendering mechanism in the performance of public-private partnerships: A transaction cost approach. *Public Management Review, 40*(1), 97–118.

Soomro, M. A., & Zhang, X. (2015). Roles of private-sector partners in transportation public-private partnership failures. *Journal of Management in Engineering, 31*(4), 04014056.

Steijn, B., Klijn, E. H., & Edelenbos, J. (2011). Public private partnerships: Added value by organizational form or management? *Public Administration, 89*(4), 1235–1252.

Teisman, G. R., & Klijn, E. H. (2002). Partnership arrangements: Governmental rhetoric or governance scheme? *Public Administration Review, 62*(2), 197–205.

Van Ham, H., & Koppenjan, J. (2001). Building public-private partnerships: Assessing and managing risks in port development. *Public Management Review, 3*(4), 593–616.

Van Slyke, D. M. (2009). Collaboration and relational contracting. In R. O'Leary & L. B. Bingham (Eds.), *The collaborative public manager: New ideas for the twenty-first century* (pp. 137–155). Washington, DC: Georgetown University Press.

Velotti, L., Botti, A., & Vesci, M. (2012). Public-private partnerships and network governance: What are the challenges? *Public Performance & Management Review, 36*(2), 340–365.

Wang, Y., & Zhao, Z. J. (2014). Motivations, obstacles, and resources: Determinants of public-private partnership in state toll road financing. *Public Performance & Management Review, 37*(4), 679–704.

Warsen, R., Klijn, E. H., & Koppenjan, J. (2019). Mix and match: How contractual and relational conditions are combined in successful public-private partnerships. *Journal of Public Administration Research and Theory, 29*(3), 375–393.

Warsen, R., Nederhand, J., Klijn, E. H., Grotenbreg, S., & Koppenjan, J.(2018). What makes public-private partnerships work? Survey research into the outcomes and the quality of cooperation in PPPs. *Public Management Review, 20*(8), 1165–1185.

Williamson, O. E. (1975). *Markets and hierarchies: Analysis and antitrust implications.* New York, NY: Free Press.

Williamson, O. E. (1981). The economics of organization: The transaction cost approach. *American Journal of Sociology, 87*(3), 548–577.

World Bank. (n.d.). *Private participation in infrastructure (PPI) project database.* Retrieved June 30, 2019, from https://ppi.worldbank.org/en/ppidata

Yang, Y., Hou, Y., & Wang, Y. (2013). On the development of public-private partnerships in transitional economies: An explanatory framework. *Public Administration Review, 73*(2), 301–310.

Yescombe, E. R. (2007). *Public-private partnerships: Principles of policy and finance.* 1st edition, Oxford, UK: Butterworth-Heinemann.

Zhang, X. (2005). Critical success factors for public-private partnerships in infrastructure development. *Journal of Construction Engineering and Management, 131*(1), 3–14.

2 Singapore-context PPPs

1 History of PPPs in Singapore

Today, Singapore is well known for being one of the most urbanized and populous cities in Asia, as it has competitive environments for investment (Gunawansa, 2010). Since its independence as a sovereign state in 1965, Singapore has expedited state-led social development to achieve the nation's political stabilization and economic success. Historically, given Singapore's unique cultures based on different races, religions, and languages, the Singapore government has played a role in harmonizing its majority traditional Chinese family culture (paternalism *per se*) with pragmatism and openness (Choy, 1987).[1] As a result, to date, Singapore has been quite stable politically with higher levels of public trust and support than its neighbors. This situation seems to be largely attributable to clearly organized hierarchical public institutions and legal frameworks accompanied by strong subsequent inducements in pursuit of modernization, urbanization, and economic growth (Choy, 1987; Hwang, Zhao, & Gay, 2013).

In addition, to achieve the label of being more pragmatic and competitive, the Singapore government has been widely open to foreign influences (especially management practices and funding by global enterprises). Tapping into relative economic freedom and ease of doing business (e.g., a lower level of corporate tax), the government has attracted a growing number of global enterprises and investors to its market (Ganguli & Ebrahim, 2017). As a result, Singapore has become a fiscally health country as well as a major financial center for the Asia Pacific region in the short term (Anwar & Ng, 2014; Ping & Trager, 2014). In particular, political leaders and statutory boards in Singapore have been most willing to adopt and implement new public policies and initiatives from Western countries (e.g., the United Kingdom) to further rapid socio-economic development (Quah, 2010). In the words of Quah (1995), "[p]olicy makers in Singapore are inclined to learn from the successes and failures of other countries and then apply the lessons to Singapore" (p. 291). As such, Singapore could become better positioned to harness its plentiful human and financial resources for innovation-oriented public reforms.

With the view that allowing the private sector to participate in public service delivery can be an efficient way to respond to the needs of citizens toward long-term physical (e.g., transportation) or environmental (e.g., water and wastewater facilities) infrastructure development and can achieve the best value for money (VFM) for government agencies, many countries have employed Public-Private Partnerships (PPPs) in their national and local projects. Since the 1980s, developing Asian countries have attempted to achieve outstanding economic performance, which, in turn, has entailed huge visible infrastructure investment and associated services (Deep, Kim, & Lee, 2019). Singapore has not been an exception to this global trend, thereby becoming one of the first Southeast Asian countries to adopt PPPs for its social infrastructure development (Han, 2016).

However, compared to neighboring countries (e.g., Indonesia, Malaysia, the Philippines, Thailand, and Vietnam), the Singapore government has not played an active role in seeking PPPs at the initial stage due to its strong economic situation (public funds are abundant) and related institutions (Deep et al., 2019). Unlike other countries (e.g., the UK), there was no urgent need in Singapore for funding from the market to invest in social infrastructure development and public projects which have mostly been run by drawing on large reserves and budget surpluses (Gunawansa, 2010; Lam, 2004; Ping & Trager, 2014). Despite the budget surpluses, Singapore struggled to tackle the Asian financial crisis, terrorism, and SARS issues in the early 2000s, and budget deficit problems surfaced for the first time in 2003 (Lam, 2004). In 2003, following other East Asian and Pacific countries (e.g., Australia, New Zealand, Indonesia, Hong Kong, China, Malaysia, Japan, Republic of Korea, and the Philippines), Singapore finally started to rely on PPPs to deliver 'non-core' government services to the people. To date, Singapore has operated its PPP projects under the control of a central government agency named the Ministry of Finance (MOF).[2]

In Singapore, the first PPP project was executed in the area of water services with the building of the Tuas Desalination Plant close to the seashore for water security and a consistent high-quality water supply (Chieh, 2017; Gunawansa, 2010; Hwang et al., 2013). The contract was awarded by the Public Utilities Board (PUB)[3] to SingSpring and is still in operation (Chieh, 2017; Gunawansa, 2010; Han, 2016). Until recently, the largest and the most complex PPP project in Singapore has been the Sports Hub (Ping & Trager, 2014). Overall, it seems that PPPs in Singapore have been slow to progress and with limited success, but they have continued to proceed in various service areas, including water and sewerage treatment, IT infrastructure, cyberspace, defense facilities, education, sports facilities, and incineration plants (Gunawansa, 2010; Han, 2016; Ping & Trager, 2014). Interestingly, the utility service areas were found to be more likely to provide evidence of the positive consequences of PPPs compared with other areas (Han, 2016).

2 Trends and features of PPPs

Infrastructure projects developed by a PPP model in Asia include the service areas of roads, rail, water, and buildings and have numbered approximately 605 in total over the period 1985–2009, which came to comprise almost 21 percent of the world's PPP projects (OECD, 2012). In terms of the status of global competitiveness and economies of infrastructure investment and development, Singapore has ranked second, preceded by Hong Kong (ranked first) from among approximately 150 Asian countries over the years 2017–2018, according to one recently published report by the Asian Development Bank and the Korean Development Institute (Deep et al., 2019). Notably, Singapore appears to be faring better than other neighboring governments in Southeast Asia (i.e., Malaysia ranked 22nd; Thailand ranked 43rd, Indonesia ranked 52nd; India ranked 66th) (Deep et al., 2019; Zen, 2018) when it comes to infrastructure development.

Another striking point is that despite the short period of time that Singapore has been implementing PPPs, compared to other ASEAN countries, it has reached an advanced level at the mature stage,[4] along with clear PPP guidelines to nurture the business environment where diverse stakeholders can engage in PPP projects in a fair and flexible manner (Deep et al., 2019; Zen & Regan, 2014). Such optimism gains support from strong financial capacity and credibility in the public and private sectors.

In Singapore, there are a total of 38 publicly known PPP projects that have been launched between the years 2000–2019.[5] Out of these 38 projects, 32 projects have been successful in terms of all the parties involved in the projects successfully fulfilling their contractual obligations. Figure 2.1 below presents a graphic overview of the successful PPP projects versus the failed PPP cases in Singapore from the years 2000–2019 in approximate percentage terms.[6] Indeed, from Figure 2.1, it can be seen that Singapore generally has enjoyed significantly more successes than failures in the area of PPPs.

Moving deeper into the successful PPP projects in Singapore, Figure 2.2 below provides a graphic illustration of the sectoral share of the 32 successful projects between the years 2000–2019 in approximate percentage terms.[7] Notably from Figure 2.2, PPP projects in the sector of residential services have had the most successful track record followed by the water and medical services sectors.

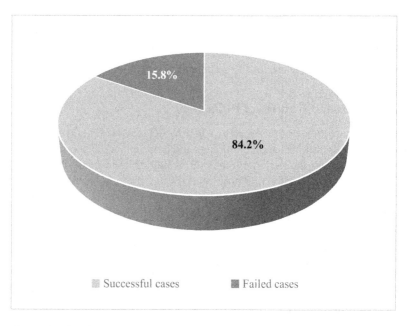

Figure 2.1 Graphic Overview of Successful versus Failed PPP Projects
Source: Authors' own elaboration

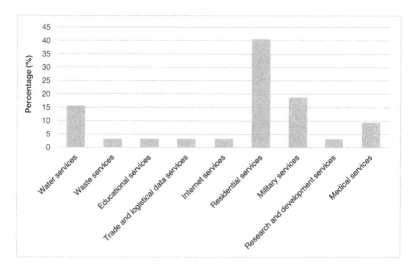

Figure 2.2 Graphic Illustration of Sectoral Share of Successful PPP Projects
Source: Authors' own calculations

3. Handbook of PPPs by the Ministry of Finance

In 2004, the Ministry of Finance (MOF) published the PPP handbook to set a comprehensive list of guidelines for the successful structure and management of PPP projects (Gunawansa, 2010; Han, 2016; Hwang et al., 2013). In 2012, this handbook was revised and a second edition was released. According to the handbook (MOF, 2012), PPPs refer to long-term partnering relationships between the public and private sectors to deliver 'non-core' government services. Specifically, it has been argued that significant sensitive service areas in Singapore, such as public security, and health and safety, will not be allowed to be compromised in the PPPs (MOF, 2012, p. 7).

In Singapore, most PPP projects tend to proceed with the Design-Build-Finance-Operate (DBFO) or the Design-Build-Operate (DBO) model (Han, 2016; MOF, 2012). Because they are recognized as a form of public procurement over a longer contract period (typically between 15 and 30 years), the Singapore government has used the Best Sourcing Framework (MOF, 2012, p. 4). In other words, before adopting the PPP model to deliver a specific public service, public agencies and managers need to ponder not only how public interests are to be protected but also how better VFM can be achieved. Therefore, there is a need to compare PPPs (the private sector is in charge of design-build-finance-operate, and the public agency purchases the services provided directly from the private sector on the most cost-effective basis) and conventional government procurement systems (i.e., contracting out: private sector builds and government operates) (MOF, 2012, p. 4; p. 27). During the entire procurement process, all stakeholders participating in a PPP project are deemed to agree to share risks, resources, and decisions in delivering public services (Chieh, 2017).

The PPP handbook is divided into four sections at large: (1) Introduction to PPPs, (2) Structuring a PPP Deal, (3) The PPP Procurement Process, and (4) Managing a PPP Relationship. In section one, the handbook discusses the definition of PPPs, typical PPP models, the underlying rationale toward adopting a PPP model in Singapore, and the roles of the public and private sectors in the PPP projects together with a rationale for the need for a PPP model and how the roles and responsibilities of main stakeholders are expected to be realized in the partnering relations. First of all, it seems that the Singapore government has continued to pursue better VFM through PPPs. PPPs are expected to help reduce the government's burden as a service provider and instead allow the government (as a service buyer) to focus on its 'core' functions and responsibilities such as policymaking and regulation (Chieh, 2017, p. 8; MOF, 2012, p. 6). Moreover, government agencies have the opportunity to use the private sector's expertise and innovation and to mitigate the risks[8] in the service delivery process by allocating them to each sector accordingly, beyond generally accepted cost-efficiency rationales. From the private sector's perspective, PPPs can be seen as an opportunity to run their business in the short term and to apply more innovative ways in pursuit of maximizing asset utilization and the commercial potential of their project in the long term (MOF, 2012, p. 7). In addition, now that PPPs basically demand collaboration and goal alignment between all stakeholders participating in the project, it will be important to better understand the primary role and responsibility of each stakeholder and how they interact with one another.

According to the PPP handbook, the main stakeholders in a PPP project typically include a public agency, service providers (private firms), equity investors and debt providers (e.g., banks and bond holders), consultants, and the Ministry of Finance (MOF, 2012, pp. 8–9). As Figure 2.3 shows, the two main participants directly engaging in a PPP project – a public agency (service purchaser) and service providers (consortium also called as special purpose vehicle) – will be held responsible for the promised outcomes. Public agencies need to specify the outcomes or outputs at the initial stage of the project and continue to monitor the service provider's progress and performance. Private firms as service providers should invest their resources and expertise to ensure a satisfactory level of public service delivery.

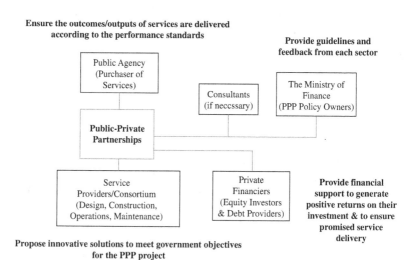

Figure 2.3 Main Stakeholders in a Typical PPP Project

Source: Author's own elaboration based on Ministry of Finance (MOF), Singapore. (2012). *Public private partnership handbook Version 2.* available at www.mof.gov.sg/Portals/0/Policies/ProcurementProcess/PPPHandbook2012.pdf

Section two provides more detailed information on how to proceed with a PPP project. Singapore PPP projects most commonly use the Design-Build-Finance-Operate (DBFO) model, and section two details some key characteristics of this model. PPPs using a DBFO model are expected to apply for long-term infrastructure contracts (up to 30 years) with a guarantee of specific, measurable outcome/outputs. Payment schedules and payments will be subject to the private sector's performance and also will be flexible based on a contingency-based approach (e.g., deductions, penalties, termination of the contract; or a binding dispute resolution procedure can take place if conflicts of interest occurs). Under the DBFO model, the PPP projects are likely to be initially financially supported by the consortium's equity investors or debt providers on the basis of capital budgeting. Later, a government agency will make a payment to the private sector as agreed (e.g., imposing user charges or fees to service users) – usually when the facility or required capacity levels are made available (MOF, 2012, p. 35). More importantly, even under the DBFO model, the private sector does not necessarily provide all of the related services for some specific cases. For example, in the case of a PPP project for schools or hospitals, business firms may construct the facilities or offer ancillary services (e.g., catering, waste management, security, and transportation), whereas the government agencies still tend to provide core services like education and healthcare services to the people (MOF, 2012, p. 13).

For successful win-win PPP deals, the role of the management team in the public sector is critical. MOF has recommended that public projects may require some organizations inside the sector, including a steering group or board (at the level of senior management or directors), a project sponsor, a project manager, and the project team (in-house staff and specialists who have expertise in financial, legal, and technical aspects), and the Centre for Public Project Management (as an advisor) (MOF, 2012, pp. 21–22). Furthermore, it has been argued that the project manager or team members should invest sufficient time and effort into planning and developing effective project management over the entire period of a PPP project. For instance, they need to ensure sufficient competition in the bidding process of the project and continue to have regular communication between (sub-) team members after awarding the contract (MOF, 2012, p. 25). On the other side of the coin, the capacity and management efforts of private firms as service providers are significant. As discussed earlier, it is expected that the private sector is ready to take on innovation, for example, in terms of introducing new ideas/technology or developing networking relationships with other stakeholders.

In the section three, the PPP procurement process that occurs prior to awarding actual contracts is explained. Basically, the procurement team must be knowledgeable at the very least about financing, specific policy/service, building development, estate management, or procurement in the public sector (MOF, 2012, p. 42). The team must aim not only to pursue cost-savings in the bidding process but also to ensure value for the money throughout the PPP. GPEs need to find the right PPP provider using transparent and efficient procurement systems. The PPP handbook describes how to proceed with actual bidding to select qualified and competent service provider(s). There are several steps in the bidding process beginning from the invitation for expressions of interest (EOI), the prequalification of bidders, a request for proposals from selected bidders, the market feedback period, issue of the final tender, to the closing of tender and awarding of the contract as shown in Figure 2.4.

First, the GPE needs to prepare the invitations for expressions of interest by conducting pre-procurement briefing sessions for available vendors who are willing to participate in the bidding process for a PPP project. Such sessions will take approximately three or six months before the issue of the PPP tender (MOF, 2012, p. 43; p. 48). The invitation will be published on the Government Electronic Business system (GeBIZ), which is a one-stop procurement online portal available to the public (MOF, 2012, p. 49). Second, after reviewing applications by the evaluation committee, a few

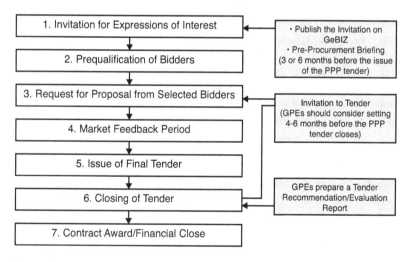

Figure 2.4 Steps in the PPP Procurement Process

Source: Author's own elaboration based on Ministry of Finance (MOF), Singapore. (2012). *Public private partnership handbook Version 2.* available at www.mof.gov.sg/Portals/0/Policies/ProcurementProcess/PPPHandbook2012.pdf

Note: Figure 2.4 was modified based on Figure 3.2.1 Flowchart of the PPP Procurement Process (see MOF, 2012, p. 47).

potential service providers are likely to be shortlisted and will become pre-qualified players. This process is intended to eliminate unsuitable bidders at the initial stage to make bidding costs as low as possible for both the private and public sector (MOF, 2012, p. 43). The bidding process must be conducted fairly according to the evaluation criteria (MOF, 2012, p. 51). Third, the actual invitation to tender (ITT) will commence with the issuing of requests for proposals from selected bidders. At this stage, the GPEs need to consider setting four or six months before the PPP tender closes. Fourth, the most significant yet salient stage of the PPP procurement process is to have a market feedback period of about three months (MOF, 2012, p. 53). During this period, the GPE and the potential bidders can be given opportunities to better understand each party's position together with their interests – what each party truly pursues and what each party is willing to provide to the PPP project. Specifically, interested parties can discuss the terms and conditions of the PPP project and contract and also exchange information and suggestions to revise the initial contract. Next, the GPE issues the final tender for the PPP project and then closes the tender along with a tender recommendation/evaluation report for final approval. Last, a PPP contract will be awarded to the service provider(s) with the most potential. The contract document signed by all stakeholders may include risk allocations and responsibilities of each main party, financial terms of the contract, and performance standards (i.e., target/due dates, deliverable quantity or quality of the service). Notably, at this stage, the provider(s) will be asked to clearly finalize all third-party agreements (e.g., in the relations with banks or subcontractors) within a timeframe, which is to reach financial close (closure) (MOF, 2012, p. 55).

The last section introduces general guidelines on how to manage effective PPP relationships. Unlike a conventional procurement model, PPPs basically require the private sector (service providers) to bring innovation to the design and construction works beyond the mere delivery of promised services. In today's uncertain and complex environment, main stakeholders participating in a long-term PPP project are easily vulnerable to financial and ethical mismanagement issues. Thus, managing PPP providers effectively is likely to play a critical role in the PPP project, particularly in situations in which the government procuring entity (GPE) is challenged to achieve expected performance goals or service effectiveness. In this respect, the PPP handbook seems to emphasize the importance of contract management (to ensure whether value for money can be delivered), performance monitoring (to diagnose whether the performance standards are met on a regular basis), and relationship management (to check whether the interests of private firms (partners *per se*) constantly remain aligned with those of government agencies over time). It concludes with some suggestions that can help the success of PPPs. For example, before proceeding with the PPP contract, clearly defined procedures and well-maintained documentation are needed as an initial significant starting point so that all stakeholders are on the same page (MOF, 2012, p. 67).

Additionally, for monitoring and management of the PPP provider's performance, the level of monitoring/evaluating work must be widely acceptable to all parties, and the quality of services delivered also should be monitored accordingly along with their quantity. Importantly, since GPE should avoid actions that could result in project risk, if possible (MOF, 2012, p. 62), relational factors such as informal communications, mutual respect and understanding between all parties should become a critical part of effective partnerships in the PPP project. Particularly in cases where there is turnover in the GPE contract management staff, it is necessary for government agencies to maintain good working relationships and build up mutual understanding and trust with their partners to minimize risks and the costs associated with misconduct (MOF, 2012, pp. 70–71).

4 Institutional and legal environments of PPPs

Contrary to expectations, the Singapore government appears to have neither independent frontline organizations nor specific laws governing PPP projects (Zen & Regan, 2014). Interestingly, however, the PPP handbook specifies that the MOF as a central government agency has overall responsibility for guiding and operating the related PPP procurement process and contracts. All government-led infrastructure projects in Singapore that cost over SGD 50 million are required to assess their 'suitability' before the government proceeds with the PPP model (Han, 2016). This conditional and strategic approach is intended to effectively take advantage of the expertise of the private sector as well as to reduce government risk (uncertainty) in the short term and financial burden on the taxpayer in the long term (Han, 2016). Specifically, an individual project team led by the government procurement entity (GPE) is likely to be formed for each project. The team is expected to be composed of managers and experts who have experience with operating and managing one or more contracts in their agencies. In addition, the Centre for Public Project Management (CP2M), which was set up in 2010, is in charge of assisting public agencies in the design and management of PPP contracts (MOF, 2012). Several evaluation committees seem to play a peripheral role in monitoring and evaluating the contractor's performance – both in quantity and quality of services delivered – and providing necessary guidance to all stakeholders.

Notes

1 Choy (1987) stated that "[p]ragmatism is seen in the modernization of traditional Chinese small businesses. It is also seen in the adoption of "foreign" practices by local and even foreign firms in Singapore, and the incorporation by foreign firms of local practices which are often very multinational in origin" (p. 141).
2 Public-Private-Partnership Legal Resource Center (PPPLRC), World Bank Group, accessed at https://ppp.worldbank.org/public-private-partnership/overview/international-ppp-units (June 25, 2019).
3 PUB is a statutory board under the Ministry of Environment and Water Resources.
4 A mature PPP policy will place greater emphasis on extracting from PPP procurement, which may take the form of improved service delivery, early delivery of projects, better utilization of infrastructure assets, construction and design innovation, and new technology. This can be achieved with greater rigor in the PPP procurement process, wider consultation with the bid market, the development of a transaction pipeline, the implementation of social infrastructure projects and availability payment streams, and formalization of viability gap funding options and governance frameworks (Zen & Regan, 2014, p. 3). In Southeast Asia, Singapore is at the mature stage; Indonesia, Malaysia, the Philippines, and Thailand are at the intermediate stage; and Cambodia, the Lao PDR, Myanmar, and Vietnam are at the initial stage (Deep, Kim, & Lee, 2019, p. 269).
5 The total number of PPP projects launched in Singapore, which includes the number of successful and failed PPP projects from the years 2000 to 2019, is drawn from a number of sources respectively. For more information on these sources, please see the sources provided in the sub-sections in Chapters 3 and 4 respectively.
6 The percentages in Figure 2.1 are calculated from the total number of PPP projects in Singapore from 2000–2019 and are rounded off to the nearest decimal point.
7 The percentages in Figure 2.2 are rounded off to the nearest decimal point and calculated from the numbers of successful PPP projects by sector. These numbers are drawn from several sources respectively. For more information on these sources, please see the sources that are provided in the sub-sections in Chapter 3 respectively.
8 According to the PPP handbook, while the private sector may deal with risks pertaining to design, construction, and financing at large, the public sector may take on political and regulatory risks (MOF, 2012, p. 6).

References

Anwar, K., & Ng, K. S. (2014). Making inroads: Capturing infrastructure opportunities in Asia. *IE Insights*, 18. Singapore: International Enterprise Singapore.
Chieh, L. W. (2017). *Policy analysis: Singapore's public-private partnerships for cybersecurity in the critical infrastructure sectors – challenges and opportunities.* Singapore: Lee Kuan Yew School of Public Policy at the National University of Singapore. Retrieved June 27, 2019, from https://lkyspp.nus.edu.sg/docs/default-source/case-studies/singapore-s-public-private-partnerships-for-cybersecurity-in-the-critical-infrastructure-sectors_challenges-and-opportunities.pdf?sfvrsn=9c38960b_2

Choy, C. L. (1987). History and managerial culture in Singapore: "Pragmatism", "openness" and "paternalism". *Asia Pacific Journal of Management, 4*(3), 133–143.

Deep, A., Kim, J., & Lee, M. (2019). *Realizing the potential of public-private partnerships to advance Asia's infrastructure development.* Manila, Philippines: Asian Development Bank, Korean Development Institute.

Ganguli, S., & Ebrahim, A. H. (2017). A qualitative analysis of Singapore's medical tourism competitiveness. *Tourism Management Perspectives, 21,* 74–84.

Gunawansa, A. (2010). Is there a need for public private partnership projects in Singapore? *COBRA 2010 – Construction, Building and Real Estate Research Conference of the Royal Institution of Chartered Surveyors.* Singapore: ScholarBank@ NUS Repository. Retrieved June 28, 2019, from https://scholarbank.nus.edu.sg/handle/10635/45950

Han, L. (2016). The problem with PPPs in Singapore: The decision to scrap a PPP for Changi Airport Terminal 5 reveals the difficulties of making this model work. *The Diplomat.* Retrieved June 28, 2019, from https://thediplomat.com/2016/09/the-problem-with-ppps-in-singapore/

Hwang, B., Zhao, X., & Gay, M. (2013). Public private partnership projects in Singapore: Factors, critical risks and preferred risk allocation from the perspective of contractors. *International Journal of Project Management, 31*(3), 424–433.

Lam, P. (2004). Public private partnerships and the search for value. *Ethos, 10*(2), 9–12. Retrieved June 26, 2019, from https://wpqr4.adb.org/LotusQuickr/copmfdr/PageLibrary482571AE005630C2.nsf/0/7B0B13BED18524A648257C3C0019CA11/$file/Day%202_Singapore%20_PPP%20Ethos%20article_WTan.pdf

Ministry of Finance (MOF), Singapore. (2012). *Public private partnership handbook: Version 2.* Retrieved June 25, 2019, from www.mof.gov.sg/Portals/0/Policies/ProcurementProcess/PPPHandbook2012.pdf

Organization for Economic Cooperation and Development (OECD). (2012). *Recommendation of the council on principles for public governance of public-private partnerships.* Retrieved June, 26, 2019, from www.oecd.org/governance/budgeting/PPP-Recommendation.pdf

Ping, T. J., & Trager, A. M. (2014). Making public-private partnerships work: Implications for Singapore and the region. *Ethos, 13,* 96–102. Retrieved June 27, 2019, from www.sais-jhu.edu/sites/default/files/ThiaJP%26ATrager%20final.pdf

Quah, J. S. T. (1995). Crime prevention in a city-state: The functions of the public police in Singapore. In K. Miyazawa & S. Miyazawa (Eds.), *Crime prevention in the urban community* (pp. 227–251). Deventer, Netherlands: Kluwer Law and Taxation Publishers.

Quah, J. S. T. (2010). *Public administration Singapore-style.* Bingley, UK: Emerald Group Publishing.

Zen, F. (2018). Public-private partnership development in Southeast Asia. *ADB Economics Working Paper Series, 553.* Retrieved July 6, 2019, from www.adb.org/sites/default/files/publication/444631/ewp-553-ppp-development-southeast-asia.pdf

Zen, F., & Regan, M. (2014). ASEAN public private partnership guidelines. *Economic Research Institute for ASEAN and East Asia.* Retrieved July 6, 2019, from https://asean.org/storage/2016/09/Public-Private-Partnership-in-South-East-Asia.pdf

3 Case studies I
Success of PPPs in Singapore

1 Introduction

Interactions between the private and public sectors in Singapore in the form of PPPs in general has increased, particularly since the 2000s, with many successful PPPs intersecting a wide variety of services. These include but are not limited to water, the internet, housing, healthcare, defense, and education. In reviewing these successful PPPs of nearly the past two decades, this study gives future PPP scholars and policy practitioners some empirically grounded case studies to consider in future PPP-related projects.

This review of successful PPP projects undertaken from the year 2000 to the 2010s contains brief descriptions of each project's background, a list of the public and private organizations involved, the specific public service being provided and the launch, execution, and post-project completion outcomes.[1]

2 Water services

Singapore has limited natural resources, especially water. Since Singapore's days as a British colony, it has heavily relied on water imports from the state of Johor in Malaysia (Singapore's northern neighbor). Malaysia has used the issue of water as political and diplomatic leverage in its dealings with Singapore. For example, Singapore's former Prime Minister Mr. Lee Kuan Yew recalled in his memoirs that Malaysia would threaten to prevent water supplies from reaching Singapore whenever disagreements arose (Nakano, 2018).

More recently, Malaysia's current Prime Minister Mahathir Mohamad in an interview criticized the price charged for the export of water by Malaysia (Nakano, 2018). He further called for a renegotiation of the water supply agreement between Singapore and Malaysia through 2061 (Nakano, 2018). This call was again echoed in March 2019 by the Johor chapter of the current Malaysian Prime Minister's *Parti Pribumi Bersatu Malaysia* (Channel News Asia, 2019).

Most concerning was the fact that the Linggiu reservoir in Johor, which provides Singapore with a significant amount of its 250 million gallons of water, was facing a very real threat of drying up in 2017 (Lin, 2019). This situation shocked many observers (Lin, 2019). Historically, Singapore's water supply has been guaranteed by Malaysia in the Separation Agreement[2] (Ministry of Foreign Affairs, Singapore, 2019). Singapore's Ministry of Foreign Affairs noted:

> Both countries have to honour the terms of the Water Agreements and the guarantee in the Separation Agreement. Neither Singapore nor Malaysia can unilaterally change them. Any breach of the Water Agreements would call into question the sanctity of the Water Agreements and the Separation Agreement, and can undermine Singapore's very existence.
> (Ministry of Foreign Affairs, Singapore, 2019)

Given this situation, it is evident that water is a key strategic resource for Singapore. Indeed, the availability of a clean and ready supply of water is crucial to maintaining Singapore's survival as a sovereign country. Therefore, ensuring a reliable, efficient, and sufficient supply of potable water in Singapore is of vital national importance to the Singapore government. This has raised the need to tap into private expertise in water treatment and water plant management. This is the primary common motivation behind all of Singapore's PPPs in the area of Water Services.

The PPP project structure that governs the water PPP projects in Singapore is known as the Design, Build, Own and Operate (DBOO) model (Fong, 2013). Under the DBOO model (see Figure 3.1), a private organization enters into a legal contract with the Public Utilities Board (PUB) to design, build, own and operate a water facility with the main aim to supply potable water to the PUB (Fong, 2013).

The PUB is a statutory board under the Ministry of the Environment and Water Resources in Singapore (PUB, 2019a). It is Singapore's national agency that is responsible for the integrated management of its water supply, water catchment, and waste water (PUB, 2019a). In the DBOO model, there are two significant agreements, namely, the Water Purchase Agreement and the Step-In-Agreement or Direct Agreement (Fong, 2013). Specifically, the Water Purchase Agreement prescribes the technical, commercial, and legal terms and conditions for the supply and purchase of water that apply to the public and private organizations in a water PPP project (Fong, 2013).

Next, the Step-In-Agreement or Direct Agreement was signed with the PUB, the appointed private water company or the concession company, and the lender or financiers (Fong, 2013). This agreement provided the lenders or financiers with the contractual right to intervene and rectify the concession company's defaults (Fong, 2013). Furthermore, it contractually enabled the PUB to intervene to ensure the continuity of the water supply (Fong,

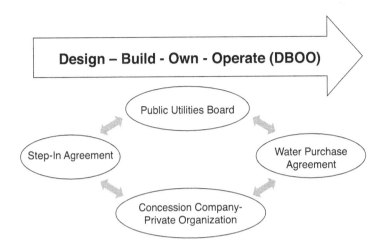

Figure 3.1 The DBOO Model

Source: Fong, H. L. (2013). *Sharing of Singapore's experience in PPP in water infrastructure projects*. Retrieved June 4, 2019, from www.slideshare.net/gwpsea/singapore-27240236?from_ action=save

Note: Figure 3.1 was a modified version of the original Design, Build, Own and Operate model by Fong (2013) under the PUB.

2013). PPP water projects in Singapore utilize either of two water treatment technologies. One is water desalination in which seawater is treated to become potable water (PUB, 2019b). The other is the NEWater production process in which used or waste water is channeled through highly advanced filtration systems to produce high-grade reclaimed water or NEWater that is suitable for industrial and household use (PUB, 2019b).

Within this context of the critical nature of the reliability of Singapore's water supply, five successful PPP water projects between 2000–2010 have been chosen for review. The reviews of these water projects are arranged in chronological order based on their project launch dates. Toward the end of this section, a summary table has been included detailing all of the reviewed water projects in chronological order.

SingSpring desalination plant project[3]

This project's objective was to engage a private entity to design, build, own and operate a water desalination plant to supply desalinated water to the PUB for 20 years. The public and private organizations involved in this project were the PUB and SingSpring (a subsidiary of Hyflux), respectively. The launch date for this project was September 2001, and its completion date was September 2005. The total cost of this project was not publicly available at the time of writing this chapter.

During this project's launch phase, the PUB awarded the contract tender to SingSpring on 19 January 2003. In its execution phase, the plant was constructed to be capable of supplying up to 136,380 m3 of desalinated potable water per day. This represents approximately 10% of Singapore's current water needs. Furthermore, SingSpring now owns and operates Singapore's first large-scale seawater desalination plant. This water plant project was the first PPP initiative in Singapore and was named by EuroMoney as the Asia Pacific Water Deal of the Year in 2003.

The SingSpring desalination plant was completed in September 2005 and commenced operations thereafter. The project's post-project completion phase has several noteworthy developments. Specifically, the plant claimed the Distinction prize for the Desalination Plant of the Year category in the Global Water Awards in 2006.

However, Hyflux became debt-laden after years of poor financial performance. In 2006, Hyflux sold off part of its stake in Singapore's first desalination plant, SingSpring, to CitySpring Infrastructure Trust (now known as Keppel Infrastructure Trust). In 2018, Hyflux supplied about 30% of Singapore's daily water requirements through desalination and recycling. Since May 2018, Hyflux suspended trading of its shares and related securities and started a court-supervised reorganization process, and subsequently Hyflux's market value fell from $2.1 billion in 2010 to $165 million in 2018.

Nevertheless, as of July 2018, Hyflux owned 30% of the plant, while Keppel Infrastructure Trust owned 70% of the plant. The original contract stipulating that the privately owned desalination plant will supply desalinated water to the PUB for 20 years, until 2025, still stands.

Ulu Pandan NEWater plant project[4]

The objective of this project was to engage a private entity to design, build, own and operate a NEWater Plant to recycle waste water and supply high-grade reclaimed water to the PUB for 20 years. This NEWater plant was constructed to fulfill water demands of the industrial and commercial sectors in western and central Singapore. The public and private organizations involved were the PUB and Keppel Seghers (part of the Keppel Infrastructure Trust), respectively. The project launch date was May 2004, and it was completed in March 2007. The total worth of this project was not available at the time of the writing of this chapter.

On 15 December 2004, the PUB awarded the tender to Keppel Seghers, which effectively marked this project's launch phase. Moving to the execution phase, the plant was equipped with a modular design and features that save space and energy. Collectively, the design and features helped lower operating costs, and the plant has been able to produce 148,000 m3 of NEWater daily. NEWater is mainly used for non-potable industrial and commercial sectors. However, a small portion of the NEWater is added to reservoir supplies before undergoing further conventional treatment by the Public Utilities Board for household consumption.

This project's completion phase saw the completion and the commencement of operations of the NEWater plant in March 2007. In 2007, the plant was the largest NEWater plant in Singapore and is now also one of the largest wastewater recycling plants worldwide. Later energy saving features that were installed in the NEWater plant included a rooftop 1 MWp solar photovoltaic (PV) power plant, which was completed in 2013. At 10,000 sqm, this rooftop solar power plant is one of the largest in Singapore and was awarded the Solar Pioneer Award in October 2012 by the Energy Innovation Programme Office led by the Singapore Economic Development Board and Energy Market Authority.

Changi NEWater plant project[5]

The objective of this project was to engage a private entity to design, build, own and operate a NEWater Plant to recycle waste water and supply 50 million gallons of high-grade reclaimed water to the PUB for 25 years. The plant would first pipe in treated used water from the Changi Water Reclamation Plant and then treat the feed water before piping the NEWater to the Public Utilities Board.

The public and private organizations involved in this project were the PUB and the Sembcorp NEWater Private Limited (a subsidiary of Sembcorp Industries), respectively. This project was launched in August 2007 and was completed in May 2010. The project's total worth was not publicly available at the time of writing this chapter.

In early 2008, the tender was awarded by the PUB to Sembcorp NEWater Private Limited. Under this contract tender, Sembcorp assumed construction and operational responsibilities for the plant. An independent accredited laboratory, together with the PUB, regularly checks the treated water quality. Furthermore, the PUB auditors conduct audits to ensure that the plant's operation and maintenance meet the specified relevant standards. On the financial side of the contract tender, the PUB pays Sembcorp NEWater Private Limited a performance-based 'tariff' for the treated water. Specifically, this tariff system has two components, namely, the fixed capacity payment and the variable output payment.

With regards to the fixed capacity payment, the board pays Sembcorp NEWater Private Limited fees cover the capital recovery charge (e.g., equity, taxes, and duties), fixed operations and management charge (e.g., salaries, overheads, and administration), and the fixed energy procurement charge. These charges are fixed regardless of the amount of NEWater the PUB purchases. However, the variable output payment stipulates that the amount paid to Sembcorp is dependent on the amount of NEWater produced by the plant. This payment covers the variable operations and management charge (e.g., spare parts, consumables, and chemicals) and the variable energy charge, namely, the variable energy cost components for power required to produce NEWater.

The execution phase of the project saw the plant being built on top of the Changi Water Reclamation Plant. This reclamation plant is one of the largest in the world. In addition, Sembcorp NEWater Private Limited installed energy-saving features such as pumps and turbo boosters to lower the plant's operational costs. The NEWater plant was completed in two phases. The first phase was completed in 2009, and the plant supplied 15 million imperial gallons (or mgd) of NEWater per day to the PUB. The second phase was completed in May 2010 and began supplying 50 mgd of NEWater a day to the PUB. By 2010, the plant had supplied about 15% of Singapore's total water needs.

BEWG-UESH NEWater plant project[6]

The objective of this project was to engage a private entity to design, build, own and operate a NEWater plant. This plant is to supply the PUB with high-grade reclaimed water for 25 years. The public organization involved is the PUB, and the private organizations involved are BEWG International Pte Ltd (subsidiary of Beijing Enterprises Water Group Limited) and UES Holdings Pte Ltd. The launch date for this project was 2014, and 2017 saw its completion. This project's worth is estimated to be 170 million dollars.

In September 2014, the PUB awarded the contract tender to the abovementioned companies to design, build, own and operate the NEWater plant. This effectively marked the launch of this project. With regard to this project's execution phase, several developments were made. Notably, the NEWater plant, as with the Changi NEWater plant, was built atop the Changi Water Reclamation Plant. The NEWater plant was awarded the Water Deal of the Year in 2016 at the Global Water Awards, which was organized by Global Water Intelligence.

Importantly, this award recognizes the plant's contribution to the enhancing private sector participation in the international water industry. The plant was constructed to be capable of producing 50 mgd of NEWater daily. This increases NEWater's ability to fulfill Singapore's daily water needs from 30% to 40%. Furthermore, the NEWater plant employs advanced purification and disinfection technology to treat wastewater.

The beginning of 2017 saw the opening of the NEWater plant. The successful completion of the plant further enhances BEWG's significant track record in water treatment. This record includes several hundred plants in China, Macau, Malaysia, Portugal, and Singapore.

The plant's completion also boosts UESH's position as an established developer, owner, and operator of water, air, waste and renewable energy assets. Moreover, it also boosts UESH's reputation as a provider of mechanical and electrical engineering services in Singapore and China.

Ulu Pandan wastewater demonstration plant project[7]

The objective of this project was to engage a private entity to design, build, own and operate a wastewater demonstration plant. This plant is responsible for testing and verifying advanced wastewater treatment technologies. The public organization involved is the PUB, and the private organizations involved are Black and Veatch + AECOMUES Holdings Pte Ltd and Mitsubishi Heavy Industries. The launch and completion dates for this project were 2015 and 2017 respectively. Once again, this project's worth was not publicly available at the time of writing this chapter.

Launch details included the design contract for the plant being awarded to Black and Veatch and AECOMUES Holdings Pte Ltd. Furthermore, Mitsubishi Corporation was named the lead contractor for this project in 2015; then Mitsubishi Heavy Industries was hired to build the plant. In the execution phase, the following development stages are highlighted: the plant was equipped with automated control systems, tanks, and other supporting systems that maximize energy efficiency.

Currently, the plant is located at the Ulu Pandan Water Reclamation Plant. The fully automated plant was built to have a water capacity of 12,500 cubic meters per day. Moreover, the plant was designed to be a training area for operators in addition to testing advanced wastewater technologies. These validated wastewater technologies will then be incorporated on a larger scale at the Tuas Water Reclamation Plant, which is scheduled to be completed in 2025. The demonstration plant opened in 2017, and its post-project completion phase saw several notable developments.

Specifically, the demonstration plant clinched the Water/Wastewater Project of the Year award at the Global Water Awards in 2018. This award was given for utilizing novel energy and manpower processes that could potentially lower energy, manpower, and land usages. Furthermore, this award recognizes the plant's creative utilization of highly advanced wastewater treatment technologies. In addition, this award underscores Singapore's strong reputation as a global hydro-hub.

Table 3.1 Summary of the Water PPP Projects in Singapore

Launch year	2001	2004	2007	2014	2015
Completion year(s)	2005	2007	2010	2017	2017
Project details	SingSpring Desalination Plant	Keppel Seghers Ulu Pandan NEWater Plant	Sembcorp Changi NEWater Plant	BEWG-UESH NEWater Plant	Ulu Pandan Wastewater Demonstration Plant

Source: Authors' own elaboration

This section on water services concludes by presenting Table 3.1 below, which summarizes the previously reviewed water PPP projects in chronological order based on their respective launch dates for ease of reference.[8]

3   Waste services

As a land-scarce country, Singapore has had to find innovative solutions to manage its waste. Notably, Singapore's growing population and economic expansion have contributed to an almost seven-fold increase in the amount of solid waste disposed of from 1,260 tons daily in 1970 to a peak of 8,559 tons daily in 2016 (National Environment Agency [NEA], 2019a). Currently, Singapore's NEA manages its solid waste as follows:

> Prior to the collection of solid waste, recyclables are sorted and retrieved for processing to prolong the lifespans of recyclable materials. The solid waste that remains is then collected and sent to the various waste-to-energy plants for incineration. . . . The incinerated ash and other non-incinerable wastes are then transported to the Tuas Marine Transfer Station . . . for the barging operation to Semakau Landfill where they are disposed of.
>
> (NEA, 2019a)

This solid waste management approach is part of a broader four-step solid waste management strategy (see Figure 3.2) in view of a projected increase in the quantity of solid waste generated as Singapore's population and the economy continues to grow (NEA, 2019b).

The NEA in Singapore designs, creates and implements Singapore's management systems for solid or general, as well as hazardous, waste. These systems include features that license and regulate waste management to ensure

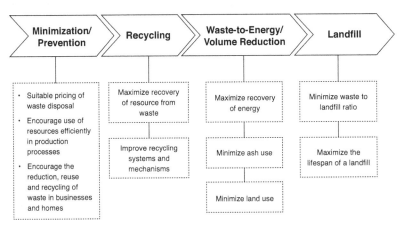

Figure 3.2 Four-Step Process of the Solid Waste Management System

Source: National Environment Agency. (2019b). *Waste management.* Retrieved July 15, 2019, from www.nea.gov.sg/our-services/waste-management/overview

Note: Figure 3.2 was a modified version of the original four-step waste management system model by the NEA (2019b).

the proper collection, treatment, and disposal of waste in Singapore (NEA, 2019b). Prior to the construction of the fifth incineration plant, Singapore had successfully built and operated four waste-to-energy plants (Keppel Seghers, 2016). Additionally, the waste collection service in Singapore was privatized in 1999 (Keppel Seghers, 2016) to introduce competition into the waste incineration sector in Singapore. This decision was made to increase the efficiency of waste services and to stimulate the development of the environment engineering industry in Singapore (Keppel Seghers, 2016). These goals laid the ideational groundwork for the fifth incineration plant project in the form of a PPP (Keppel Seghers, 2016).

Fifth incineration plant project[9]

This project was based on the DBOO model, which is similar to that used to guide the design and implementation of the water PPP projects reviewed in the previous section. However, this DBOO model included two agreements that were specific to this project: the 'take-or-pay' agreement and the incineration services agreement. Under the 'take-or-pay' agreement, the NEA was contractually obliged to the private company to purchase 100% of the incineration volume at a tender-established price. Furthermore, the NEA was to be responsible for the demand risks by granting the plant operator full capacity payment, regardless of the plant's actual utilization rate. Next, the incineration services agreement contractually ensured that the delivery of incineration services was done through initiatives that included, but were not limited to, technical requirements and commercial terms and conditions.

The main objective of this project was to engage a private organization to design, build, own, and operate an incineration plant to incinerate solid waste daily for the NEA for a period of 25 years. The public and private organizations involved in this project were the NEA and Keppel Seghers, respectively. The launch date of this project was May 2005, and the plant became operational from 2009, when the project was completed. This project's worth was not publicly available at the time of writing this chapter.

The project was launched with the tender contract being awarded to Keppel Seghers on 14 November 2005. This plant holds the honor of being the first PPP initiative between the NEA and the private sector. The project execution phase, which began in 2006, saw the plant being equipped with the Keppel's in-house technology. Specifically, the plant was designed to utilize combustion grate and flue gas cleaning proprietary technologies. With these technologies, the plant's incineration capability stood at 800 tons of solid waste daily and could generate 22 megawatts of environmentally friendly energy. Consequently, 90% of the waste volume could be reduced. The plant occupies 1.6 hectares of land, making it one of the world's smallest waste-to-energy plants in terms of land mass. Collectively with the other waste-to-energy plant in Senoko, Keppel Seghers is able to burn up to 47.6% of Singapore's incinerable waste.

The project was completed and the plant has been operational since October 2009. Upon completion, Keppel's estimated revenue from the incineration plant was 450 million dollars over the next 25 years of the contract tenure. Importantly, since October 2009, the plant has been operated by Keppel Seghers without any major incidents.

4 Educational services

Facing the reality of a scarcity of natural resources, Singapore has turned to developing a robust education sector to drive economic growth and development since 1965. Indeed, from 1965, Singapore has transformed itself from a country with no compulsory education and only a small number of pre-university and university graduates and skilled workers to a country that regularly tops global education indexes (Organisation for Economic Co-operation and Development [OECD], 2010, p. 160).

For instance, students in Singapore were among the global top achievers in mathematics and science in the Trends in International Math and Science

Study in 1995, 1999, 2003, and 2007 (OECD, 2010, p. 160). Furthermore, Singapore ranked fourth in the area of literacy in the Progress in International Reading Literacy Study in 2006 and was among the ranks of top-performing countries in the PISA survey in 2009 (OECD, 2010, p. 160).

More recently, Singapore has topped the World Bank's Human Capital Index (HCI), which measures the relationship between education, health, productivity, and economic growth (Yulisman, 2018). According to the World Bank, Singapore's HCI demonstrated that its investments in its people's education and health will currently result in children born in Singapore having the ability to fulfill 88% of their potential to be productive at age 18, assuming that they receive full education and possess good health (Yulisman, 2018).

An example of such education investments is Singapore's approach to post-secondary education in the Institute of Technical Education (ITE). The ITE was established in 1992 as a post-secondary educational institution under Singapore's Ministry of Education (ITE, 2011). The ITE primarily provides career and technical education and is also an important developer of the national occupational skills certification and standards to boost Singapore's labor competitiveness (ITE, 2011). Notably, ITEs in Singapore are renowned for their broad-scoped, multidisciplinary curriculum and an educational approach that emphasizes the intellectually rigorous development and application of technical-practical skills in the workforce in a socially responsible manner (PricewaterhouseCoopers [PwC], 2010).

Furthermore, the "One ITE System, Three Colleges" education and governance model comprises three institutions, namely, ITE College Central, ITE College East, and ITE College West (ITE, 2011). Also, Singapore's Ministry of Finance (MOF) in its 2004 PPP handbook promoted the utilization of the PPP model for projects worth above 50 million dollars (PwC, 2014). Indeed, to continually develop Singapore's post-secondary education system with the ultimate goal of driving Singapore's future economic development there is a need to develop physical educational infrastructure that encourages innovative and creative thinking at the post-secondary level to solve real world problems effectively. Building such an infrastructure calls for engagement with the private sector to draw on its expertise in building, financing, and operating educational infrastructure. This need for engagement, coupled with the earlier advice of the MOF on pursuing PPP projects (PwC, 2014), laid the policy groundwork for the PPP, ITE college west project.

ITE college west project[10]

This project's main objective was to engage a private company to design, build, finance, and operate the college for 27 years. Under the Design, Build, Finance and Operate (DBFO) model that this project utilizes, PwC, as the project group's financial advisor, led the project group, which consisted of legal and technical advisors, throughout the project term until the college was completed. Notably, the PwC-led advisory body helped ITE narrow down the list of bidders and consortiums which were made up of companies dealing with the management of finance, construction, architecture, and facilities.

These efforts were made to support this project's other objectives, which included ITE's expectation of the college's design function and exterior to be aesthetically pleasing and also to produce the financial benefits for which PPPs are renowned. The public organization involved was the ITE (under Singapore's Ministry of Education), and the private organizations involved were PwC (financial advisor), Gammon Capital (builder of the college) and DP Architects (architect of the college). This project was launched in July 2006 and was completed in 2010. This project's worth was almost 400 million dollars.

The tender contract was awarded on 11 August 2008, after which the construction of the college began, marking the execution phase of this project. The ITE college west project holds the distinction of being Singapore's first PPP project in the education sector. Spanning a land area of 9.54 hectares, this college has a gross floor area of 114,480 m^2. The college's architectural design is a combination of education with urban architectural principles, landscape design, and environmentally friendly engineering.

Furthermore, the college is equipped with a variety of learning, food, exercising, and entertainment facilities that can cater to 7,200 full-time and 8,100 part-time students, and 630 staff members. In addition, the college's environmentally friendly features can produce approximated savings of 8,021,188 kWh per year in energy and 48,785 m^3 per year in water consumption.

Between the years 2009–2010, the college won several awards, including but not limited to the Asia Pacific PPP Deal of the Year by Project Finance International, Singapore, and it held a spot in the world's top 100 most interesting infrastructure projects listed in KPMG Global's *Infrastructure Practice/Infrastructure Journal*. In July 2010, the college was completed, marking the completion phase of this project. The post-project completion phase of this project saw the college clinching the "Top Achiever Award 2010/2011" in the Singapore Environmental Achievement Awards offered by the Singapore Environment Council.

5   Trade and logistical services

Singapore's role as a trading hub stems from its colonial past as an entrepot trading post under the British empire. Since 1965, the Singapore government has made significant policy moves to drive economic development. A notable example of such policy moves is the adoption of export-oriented industrialization (Menon, 2015). From 1985 to 2010, the modern services industry such as info-communications, financial and business services increasingly became a significant driver of Singapore's economic growth, increasing from 24% of Singapore's GDP in 1985 to 28% in 2010 (Menon, 2015).

Furthermore, as Singapore took steps to transit to a knowledge-based economy in 1999, the economic development board launched its economic master plan for Singapore in the 21st century, which is known as 'Industry 21' (Pek, 2017). This master plan laid out the strategic plans for nine industry clusters that included logistics, communications and media, headquarters, and business services (Pek, 2017). From 2000 to 2015, innovation, knowledge, research, and development have been the focal sectors driving economic development (Pek, 2017).

In addition to these policy initiatives, the Singapore government, by building effective trading facilities, has positioned Singapore to be the most important commodities trading center in Asia (Tay, 2015) as well as the largest commodity trading hub in Asia (Chia, 2017; SBS Consulting, 2019). Overall, Singapore's GDP grew from almost 975 million USD in 1965 to about 364 billion USD in 2018 (World Bank, 2019a).

In this export-led growth picture, arguably at least since 2000, the Singapore government has had to ensure effective and secure information exchange between the various sectors that were crucial to driving this export-led economic development. This called for the need to engage with private expertise on large-scale information management know-how to facilitate that information exchange. Importantly, this need formed the policy backdrop for the TradeXchange project to be established.

TradeXchange project[11]

The objective of this project was to engage a private entity to develop, operate, and maintain an integrated information system for the trading and logistics sectors for ten years. The public and private organizations involved were Singapore Customs and CrimsonLogic Pte Ltd, respectively. This project was launched in December 2005 and was completed in November 2007. This project's worth was publicly unavailable at the time of writing this chapter.

Notably, the contract was awarded to CrimsonLogic Pte Ltd on 8 December 2005. In the execution phase of this project, the integrated information system was designed to provide a single electronic platform for combined work processes, submissions, and enquiries to the seaports, airports, maritime, customs, and controlling authorities (Taher, Yang & Kankanhalli, 2012).

In 2007, the system was made operational and CrimsonLogic Pte Ltd was contractually required to operate and maintain the information system for ten years until 2017. Notably, this project's post-project completion phase saw some critical points. Specifically, during the ten-year operation and maintenance tenure by CrimsonLogic Pte Ltd, the Singapore government would own the information and data gathered by agencies due to statutory and regulatory requirements. Furthermore, commercial data would continue to be under the ownership of the companies that created that data. Also, permission to share the data was to be obtained from that data's owner.

6   Internet services

In a knowledge-based economy, an information infrastructure that is able to effectively support transactions of large data sets is vital to drive economic development. Indeed, broadband technology has been a critical factor in enabling Singapore to be competitive in the global knowledge-based economy (Info-communications Development Authority of Singapore [IDA], 2009). Therefore, broadband as an infrastructure serves as a source of competitive advantage and is not a luxury feature (IDA, 2009).

Historically, Singapore has continued to invest in info-communications infrastructure to prevent economic growth from being restricted by infrastructural constraints (IDA, 2009). For example, in the late 1980s, the Singapore government invested in a fully digital telephone network that could work faster than the required 9600 bps at that time, and the mid-1990s saw the telephone and cable TV networks upgraded to broadband, once again operating faster than the required 56Kbps (IDA, 2008). From the mid to late 2000s, there was increasing demand for broadband as well as a demand for greater information processing speeds in Singapore (IDA, 2008). Furthermore, the Peer-to-Peer (P2P) sector experienced a tremendous percentage growth in terms of internet traffic from the late 1990s onward until 2006 (CacheLogic, n.d.).

In light of these changing economic and info-communication trends, the move to continually keep Singapore at the forefront of info-communications technology required the construction of a technologically advanced communication network infrastructure. In order to proceed with this construction, endeavor efficiently and within budget, there was a great deal of incentive for the Singapore government to draw on private expertise in the design and build of complex info-communication infrastructure. This led to the next generation national broadband network project. The Singapore government argued that this new network would create a dynamic broadband sector in which high-speed broadband networks that operate at affordable prices would enable new educational practices such as teaching and

learning via internet video conferencing (IDA, 2009). New internet entertainment services such as on-demand television as well as lower internet
connectivity cost were also made possible (IDA, 2009). This lower cost
would create an economic incentive for small and medium enterprises to
utilize info-communications and technology in Singapore (IDA, 2009),
which could enhance their long-term economic productivity and contribute
to Singapore's long-term economic growth.

Next generation national broadband network project[12]

The Singapore government pursued this project in two distinct stages. First,
they initiated a competitive dialogue with 12 prequalified private-sector
organizations in the second stage of the project, namely the Request for Pro-
posal (RFP) stage. The competitive dialogue phase was a platform for the
Singapore government to better understand the perspectives of the private
sector on key RFP components, the effective open access industry structure
and the interconnection offer concept that the operators proposed.

Under the RFP stage of the project, the open access industry structure
consisted of three tiers. At the bottom tier of this structure, the Network
Company (NetCo) would be responsible for the design, construction, and
operation of this project's passive infrastructure, which would include opti-
cal fiber cables. Moving up to the middle tier, the Operating Company
(OpCo) would be responsible for the design, construction, and operation of
this project's active infrastructure, which would comprise routers, switches,
and access network equipment. Therefore, the main objectives of this project were to engage private entities to design, build, and operate the passive infrastructure and active infrastructure of the new national broadband
network. The public organization involved was the Info-communications
Development Authority of Singapore (IDA), and the private organizations
involved were OpenNet Consortium (NetCo) and Nucleus Connect (OpCo).
The launch of this project took place in February 2006. The passive infrastructure was completed in 2009, and the active infrastructure was completed in 2010. There was no publicly available project worth at the time of
writing this chapter.

In September 2008, the Singapore government awarded the NetCo project contract to OpenNet Consortium and, in April 2009, awarded the OpCo
project contract to Nucleus Connect. The OpenNet consortium consisted of
Axia NetMedia Corporation (30% share), Singapore Telecommunications
Limited (30% share), Singapore Press Holdings Limited (25% share) and
SP Telecommunications Pte Ltd (15% share). During the execution phase of
this project, the new national broadband network was expected to cover 60%
of businesses and homes in Singapore by 2010 and 95% of all businesses

and homes by mid-2012. Notably, these execution timelines were ahead of the Singapore government's initial country-wide network installation target by 2015 as the laying of passive infrastructure was done using existing ducts and manholes to minimize the degree of physical construction work required. In August 2009 and August 2010, the passive and active infrastructure were completed, respectively. In this project's post-project completion phase, fiber broadband plans capable of speeds starting from 100 megabits per second have been available to businesses and consumers at competitive prices. Universal service obligations for both OpenNet consortium and Nucleus Connect were to begin in January 2013.

7 Residential services

From 1990 to 2011, Singapore's GDP per capita, Purchasing Power Parity, which is a unit used to measure per capita income of a country, rose from almost 23,000 current international dollars to about 100,000 current international dollars (World Bank, 2019b). In recognition that Singaporeans were experiencing higher disposable income levels as evidenced by this rise in per capita income, as well as the changing demands of Singaporeans in general, the Singapore government launched the Design, Build and Sell Scheme (DBSS) flat project (National Library Board, Singapore [NLB], 2014). This project to construct residential dwellings aimed to include the private sector in the construction of flats to enable Singapore's government authority on housing matters, the Housing and Development Board (HDB), to deemphasis its builder role and focus on regulating the public housing market (NLB, 2014). Thirteen DBSS flats were successfully completed during the years 2005–2011 (HDB, 2018). In the words of HDB, the DBSS flats were: "built by private developers with each development characterized by unique external features" (HDB, 2018). These unique features included, but were not limited to, attractive architectural design elements of the flats.

Under the DBSS project's PPP model, the private developers were invited to bid for the open land tender contract (NLB, 2014). Upon winning the tender, the private developers were responsible for designing, building, selling (Chua, 2005, p. 5), and maintaining the flats (NLB, 2014). However, there were certain caveats attached to these responsibilities.

First, during the building phase, although the private developers had more freedom in terms of flat design, size, type, and physical configuration, they had to abide by the HDB's public housing guidelines pertaining to the residences' "open concept, building quality and safety and avoidance of facilities that are expensive to maintain" (NLB, 2014). Second, with regard to selling the flats, the private developers had the freedom to determine prices, albeit reflecting binding guidelines that were imposed by the Monetary Authority of

Table 3.2 Summary of the 13 DBSS Flat Projects

Launch date	Completion date	Project name
28 October 2005	15 December 2008	The Premiere@ Tampines
16 March 2007	11 January 2011	City View @ Boon Keng
12 September 2007	27 July 2011	Park Central @ AMK
27 December 2007	15 August 2011	Natura Loft @ Bishan
8 April 2008	28 February 2011	Parc Lumiere @ Simei
27 June 2008	24 April 2011	The Peak @ Toa Payoh
31 March 2010	2013	Adora Green
23 June 2010	June 2014	Centrale 8 @Tampines
14 September 2010	3 November 2014	Belvia
12 October 2010	October 2014	Parkland Residences
16 November 2010	4 September 2014	Lake Vista@Yuan Ching
26 January 2011	2015	Trivelis
16 March 2011	May 2015	Pasir Ris One

Source: Authors' own elaboration

Singapore (The Business Times, 2005, p. 3). Third, on the issue of flat maintenance, the private developers were responsible for any building defects for up
to one year, but maintenance of the common grounds and public parking lots
of the building estate would be under the town council's jurisdiction (NLB,
2014). Notably, the DBSS flats have HDB-administered land leases of 99
years, which begin when the flats are completed (NLB, 2014). For ease of reference, toward the end of this section, Table 3.2 summarizes the 13 DBSS flat
projects in chronological order in terms of the flats' respective launch dates.[13]

The DBSS flat projects[14]

The *Premiere @ Tampines* project was launched on 28 October 2005, and the
tender was awarded to Sim Lian Land Pte Ltd on 18 January 2006. Construction of the project took place along Tampines Avenue 6 and was completed
on 15 December 2008 with 616 residential units. The post-project completion phase of this project saw it earn the distinction of being the first DBSS
flat project in Singapore. This project's worth stood at 82,222,000 dollars.

The *City View @ Boon Keng* DBSS project was launched on 16 March
2007, and the tender was awarded on 6 June 2007 to three companies,
namely, Hoi Hup Realty Pte Ltd, Sunway Concrete Products (S) Pte Ltd
and Oriental Worldwide Investments Inc. The flats were built along Boon
Keng Road and were completed on 11 January 2011 with 714 residential
units. This group of units was the second in the line of DBSS projects that
were built, and its worth totaled 170,200,000 Singapore dollars.

On 12 September 2007, the *Park Central @ AMK* DBSS project was launched and the tender was awarded to Greatearth Developments Pte Ltd on 5 December 2007. The residences were constructed along Ang Mo Kio Street 52 and were completed on 27 July 2011. This development was the third DBSS project to be built, with a value of 134,180,000 Singapore dollars.

The launch date for the *Natura Loft @ Bishan* project was 27 December 2007 and the tender was awarded to Qingdao Construction Group Corporation (Singapore Branch) on 28 February 2008. This project was built along Bishan Street 24 and was completed on 15 August 2011. Upon completion, the development became the fourth DBSS project to be successfully completed and the project worth was 135,888,777 Singapore dollars.

The *Parc Lumiere @ Simei* project was launched on 8 April 2008, and Sim Lian Land Pte Ltd was awarded the tender contract on 6 June 2008. Construction of these units took place along Simei Road and was completed on 28 February 2011 with a total of 360 residential units being built. This project was the fifth DBSS project to be completed since 2005, and its worth stood at 52,000,000 Singapore dollars.

On 27 June 2008, *The Peak @ Toa Payoh* project launch commenced, and three private corporations were awarded tender on 22 August 2008. These corporations were Hoi Hup Realty Pte Ltd, Sunway Developments Pte Ltd, and Hoi Hup JV Development Pte Ltd. The residences were built along Lorong 1A Toa Payoh and were completed on 24 April 2011 comprising 1,203 units. Being the sixth DBSS project to be built, its worth stood at 198,822,000 Singapore dollars.

The *Adora Green* project saw its launch on 31 March 2010, and two private companies, namely, Guthrie (DBP) Pte Ltd and SK Land Pte Ltd were awarded the tender on 24 May 2010. Built near Yishun Avenue 11 and Yishun Central, the project was completed in 2013 with 806 residential units. As the seventh DBSS project to be completed, its worth totaled 148,888,888 Singapore dollars.

Launched on 23 June 2010, the tender contract for the *Centrale 8 @ Tampines* project was awarded to Sim Lian Land Pte Ltd on 6 August 2010. Construction of the units took place near Tampines Avenue 5 and Tampines Central 8 and were completed in June 2014 with 708 residential units. The flat was the eighth DBSS project to be completed in Singapore, and the project's worth amounted to 178,128,000 Singapore dollars.

The *Belvia* project was launched on 14 September 2010, and the tender was awarded to CEL Development Pte Ltd on 4 November 2010. Built along Bedok Reservoir Crescent, the project was completed on 3 November 2014 with 488 residential units. This project was the ninth in the line of DBSS projects being built, with a worth of 112,688,000 Singapore dollars.

Commencement of the *Parkland Residences* project launch began on 12 October 2010, and the tender was awarded to Kwan Hwee Investment

Pte Ltd on 2 December 2010. Constructed along Upper Serangoon Road, the flats were completed in October 2014 with 680 residential units. Being the ninth DBSS project, its worth was valued at 155,228,998 Singapore dollars.

On 16 November 2010, the *Lake Vista @ Yuan Ching* project was launched, and the tender was awarded to three companies, namely, Hoi Hup Realty Pte Ltd, Sunway Developments Pte Ltd, and SC Wong Holdings Pte Ltd on 10 January 2011. The flats were built along Yuan Ching Road and saw completion on 4 September 2014 with 682 residential units. It was the eleventh DBSS project and its worth stood at 131,600,000 Singapore dollars.

The *Trivelis* project was launched on 26 January 2011, and the tender was awarded to EL Development Pte Ltd on 10 March 2011. Constructed along Clementi Avenue 4, the units were completed in 2015 with 888 residences. This project was the twelfth DBSS project, and its worth was 224,000,000 Singapore dollars.

On 16 March 2011, the *Pasir Ris One* project was launched, and the tender was awarded to two companies, namely, Singxpress Land (Pasir Ris) Pte Ltd and Kay Lim Holdings Pte Ltd on 3 June 2011. Built near Pasir Ris Central and Pasir Ris Drive 1, the project was completed on May 2015 with 447 residential units. Being the thirteenth DBSS project, this project's worth stood at 123,880,009 Singapore dollars.

8   Military services

In 1967, the Singapore government instituted National Service (NS), which is a compulsory military service duty that conscripts all eligible Singapore male citizens for about two years (NLB, 2015). This policy was implemented in light of Singapore's reality as a country with a small population base and the need for a strong defense force. Since then, NS is a legal obligation of eligible male Singaporean permanent residents. Several decades later, Singapore's Ministry of Defence (MINDEF) published a comprehensive e-book in which it argued that the coming 21st century would see the strategic landscape remaining dynamic as countries sought to adjust to the strategic trends in a post-Cold War era (MINDEF, 2000a, p. 2). Consequently, this would bring about new challenges for the defense of Singapore (MINDEF, 2000a, p. 2).

In policy terms, this meant that Singapore would continue to pursue diplomacy and build a strong defense to protect its survival and success as the 21st Century comes into fruition (MINDEF, 2000a, p. 2). More specifically, MINDEF and the Singapore Armed Forces planned an increase in Singapore's defense strength so that Singapore would be well prepared to meet any future challenges (MINDEF, 2000a, p. 2).

Furthermore, the Singapore government strongly believed that in the area of military security, stronger global cooperation was required to address the diverse and complicated security challenges that the international community would encounter in the 21st century (MINDEF, 2000a, p. 3). Moving on to military technology in particular, MINDEF argued that:

> We are witnessing a revolution in military affairs . . . [a]dvances in weapons technology that are equipped with electronic information systems drive the current revolution . . . [t]o stay ahead, we need to keep on building up and maintaining a technological capability . . . [and] as a small and resource-scarce nation . . . [Singapore faces] a challenge for which new and creative solutions need to be found continuously.
>
> (MINDEF, 2000b, pp. 10–11)

Situated within this changing global strategic and military environment, there was a strong incentive for MINDEF to draw from the private military sector's technological expertise and know-how. Doing so would enable MINDEF to develop innovative and effective solutions to enhance its defense capabilities. With this in mind, the military PPP projects in Singapore were born. This section reviews six such projects and ends with Table 3.3, which summarizes these projects in chronological order based on their respective launch/tender awarded dates.[15]

Military PPP training courses[16]

Transport winged course

In 2003, Singapore Technologies Aerospace Ltd (ST Aerospace) was awarded the tender contract for the transport wing course. Under this contract, ST Aerospace was also responsible for using the modified King Air

Table 3.3 Summary of the Military PPP Projects

Launch/tender awarded date	Completion date	Project name
2003	Not available	Transport winged course
August 2005	2008	Basic wings course
November 2005	2006	Rotary winged course
December 2005	May 2006	NS portal
2008	Not available	Flying instruction project
Not available	2010	Rifle range management project

Source: Authors' own elaboration

C-90 Beechcraft as per the Republic of Singapore Air Force (RSAF)'s special training requirements to provide training for the RSAF's trainee pilots until they became fully qualified transport pilots.

Basic wings course

Next, in August 2005, the launch of the basic wings course project began and the tender was awarded to Pilatus Aircraft Ltd and Lockheed Martin in November 2006. Specifically, Pilatus Aircraft Ltd would supply 19 PC-21 advanced turboprop trainer aircrafts for the RSAF's basic wings course from 2008–2028. During this period, these 19 aircraft would form part of a training package that was awarded to Lockheed Martin Simulation, Training and Support under the Lockheed Martin company, which would operate the basic winged course for the RSAF in that time period as well. The execution phase for this project saw military training for this course being conducted at the Royal Australian Air Force Base at Pearce in Australia. Furthermore, this PPP contract facilitated the provision of ground-based pilot and weapons system operator equipment, flight-simulator hours, and flying. Significantly, this PPP project holds the honor of being one of the first PPP training systems in the world.

Rotary winged course

Later in November 2005, the tender for another military PPP training project, the rotary winged course, was awarded to ST Aerospace. Under this contract, ST Aerospace would supply MINDEF with five EC120 Colibri helicopters and provide these helicopters complete technical and logistic support for 20 years from 2006–2026. Furthermore, ST Aerospace would be contractually liable to own and maintain the five helicopters for MINDEF during those 20 years. This contract has an estimated worth of 120 million dollars.

Flying instruction project

In addition, ST Aerospace also won a 105 million-dollar contract for a flying instruction project from MINDEF. Under this contract, ST Aerospace would provide RSAF with the aircraft and training instructors to meet the RSAF's training requirements from 2012–2032. Also, as part of this contract, ST Aerospace would acquire and maintain a Gulfstream 550 aircraft.

NS portal PPP project [17]

The contract for the NS portal project was awarded by MINDEF to the NCS Group in December 2005. Under this contract, the NCS Group was responsible for developing, maintaining, and operating the NS portal over the next five years. Furthermore, this contract included providing and enhancing the NS portal, data center, and a 24-hour call center.

In a nutshell, the NS portal enables NS military personnel to access more than 130 specific NS linked and other lifestyle online services to help them effectively balance lifestyle, work, and learning. This portal is a single platform for Singapore Armed Forces (SAF), Singapore Police Force (SPF) and Singapore Civil Defence Force (SCDF), and shares common touch-points such as the portal URL, call center number and SMS number. The project was completed in May 2006, and SPF and SCDF transferred their NS services to the NS Portal in late October 2006.

Rifle range management project[18]

In late 2010, the SAF together with private operators operationalized the project that would see the latter party operating the SAF's 14 outdoor rifle firing ranges. Specifically, the private commercial operators would assume the repair of the ranges, the tracking of scores, and the retrieval of used bullet cartridges. These rifle firing ranges are located in Nee Soon, Mandai, Poyan, Safti, and Pulau Tekong. With lengths of between 25m and 500m, these ranges are used by the SAF for live-firing practice involving small weapons.

9   Research and development services

From 2006 to 2016, Singapore's role as a manufacturing hub saw a boost when its manufacturing output and value added to the rest of the economy grew annually at a compounded growth rate of 1.1% and 2.3% respectively (Agency for Science, Technology and Research [A*STAR], 2017, p. 5). Furthermore, in 2005, every S$1 of manufacturing value added led to the creation of an additional S$0.25 of value added to the rest of the economy (A*STAR, 2017, p. 5). By 2012, additional value added to the rest of the economy had grown to S$0.34 as manufacturing increased engagement with other sectors, especially with but not limited to business services (A*STAR, 2017, p. 5). Under such growing trends in Singapore's manufacturing sector, the Singapore government needed to increase research and industry partnerships with the private manufacturing sector to further reinforce the role of manufacturing as an important driver of Singapore's economic development into the future. With these objectives in mind, the Advanced Remanufacturing Technology Centre (ARTC) project came into being.

ARTC PPP project[19]

In June 2012, the Agency for Science, Technology and Research (A*STAR) and Nanyang Technological University partnered to establish a research center that specializes in testing and developing manufacturing technologies.

This project sought to overcome technological gaps in the process of adopting advanced remanufacturing techniques. Housed in the Jurong Town Corporation CleanTech Two building, the Advanced Remanufacturing Technology Centre (ARTC) was completed on 28 January 2015. Upon completion, ARTC held the distinction of being Asia's first remanufacturing research establishment to be built under a PPP initiative. During the center's opening in 2015, second Minister for trade and industry and home affairs Mr. S Iswaran commented on the center's research and development capabilities:

> ARTC will be a game-changer for the remanufacturing sector in Singapore. It seeks to develop capabilities which will help companies in the aerospace, oil and gas, energy and automotive industries tackle the high component costs through remanufacturing.
>
> (Teng, 2015)

The notable achievements of post-project completion include that the center has become a platform for collaborative research between A*STAR, NTU, and over 29 local and global private industry firms, such as Rolls-Royce and Singapore Aero Engine Services.

10   Medical services

During a lecture at Singapore Management University in 2015, Singapore's Prime Minister Lee Hsien Loong highlighted that Singapore's aging population would bring about complex societal problems and that its effects were already being felt (Today, 2015b). Specifically, Prime Minister Lee remarked:

> Based on trends, if we project into 2050, even with immigration, the population pyramid will be inverted ... [w]e are going to be growing old faster than any society in the world. .... Who will pay the taxes, to spend on whom? How do we keep (the economy) prosperous, vibrant and forward looking? Who will man the Singapore Armed Forces and defend us?
>
> (Today, 2015b)

Indeed, the number of Singapore citizens aged 65 and above is growing rapidly, from 220,000 in 2000 to 440,000 in 2015 and is expected to increase to 900,000 by 2030 (Today, 2015b). This is compounded by the fact that Singapore's total population growth was only 1.3 percent in 2014, which was at its slowest pace since 2005, and the total fertility rate has continued to drop despite the government's benefits and encouragement (Today, 2015b). In 2017, further estimates predict that in about three decades, the number of Singapore citizens aged 65 and above will comprise 47% of Singapore's

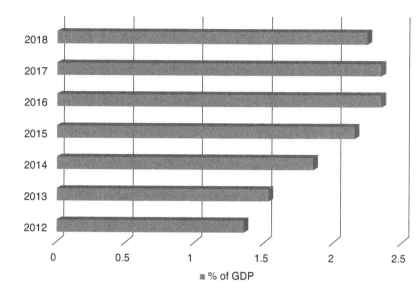

Figure 3.3 Healthcare Expenditure as a % of GDP in Singapore

Source: Singapore Business Review. (2018). *Healthcare spending is shifting from hospital-building to maintenance.* Retrieved July 18, 2019, from https://sbr.com.sg/healthcare/in-focus/healthcare-spending-shifting-hospital-building-maintenance

Note: Figure 3.3 is a modified version of the original graph reflecting the healthcare expenditure as a percentage of GDP in Singapore by the Singapore Business Review (2018).

total population (Siau, 2017). In light of such age demographic projections, the proportion of Singapore's healthcare expenditure as a percentage of GDP (see Figure 3.3) has grown from almost 1.50% in 2012 to 2.50% in 2017 (Singapore Business Review, 2018).

With a rapidly aging population, followed by a rise in healthcare spending, there was a need to devise innovative solutions that would enhance the effectiveness and efficiency as well as affordability of medical healthcare in Singapore. This called for collaboration with private medical expertise to aid medical healthcare delivery in Singapore. Three medical PPP projects were set up that will be reviewed below. At the end of this section, Table 3.4 will summarize the reviewed medical PPP projects in chronological order for ease of reference.[20]

Medical PPP projects [21]

The Community Health Assist Scheme (CHAS) was introduced to the general public in Singapore by Singapore's Ministry of Health (MOH) in 2012. This scheme was the result of a collaboration between MOH and several

Table 3.4 Summary of the Medical PPP Projects

Launch date	Completion date	Project name
Not available	2012	CHAS
December 2014	3 June 2015	ECC
Not available	December 2017	Thomson Celebrating Life program

Source: Authors' own elaboration

private medical clinics in Singapore. Under the CHAS, Singapore citizens from lower- to middle-income households, as well as all citizens aged about 65 and above, are eligible to receive subsidies for medical and dental care at participating general practitioner and dental clinics. Also, CHAS recipients enjoy subsidized medical referrals to specialist outpatient clinics that are located at public hospitals and subsidized dental referrals to the Singapore's national dental center when required.

On 3 June 2015, the Raffles Medical Group, another private medical healthcare provider in Singapore, together with MOH, made the Emergency Care Collaboration (ECC) service available to the Singapore public. The ECC project was first launched in December 2014 and was designed to enhance access to subsidized medical healthcare in Singapore. Under this collaboration, Raffles Hospital provides critical medical care to patients sent there by the Singapore Civil Defence Force (SCDF) ambulances at subsidized prices. In addition, the hospital provides medical care services for patients who need to be admitted for subsequent inpatient care or are referred to specialist outpatient units at subsidized rates.

In December 2017, the Thomson Medical Group, a private medical health-care provider in Singapore, in conjunction with Singapore's Health Promotion Board (HPB), operationalized the Thomson Celebrating Life program. This program includes a mobile application that is linked to the Singapore Health Promotion Board (HPB)'s HealthHub for health articles. Furthermore, the app shares the medical group's internal articles with HPB. Perhaps most importantly, the app will enable Thomson Medical patients to monitor their own medical and health records. The post-project completion phase of this project saw it being highlighted as the first PPP initiative with the HPB.

Notes

1 In this chapter, we include financial and/or logistical and/or administrative details of the projects that are publicly available online. It is important to note that some of those details may be withheld by the relevant public and/or private organizations for reasons potentially including, but not limited to, contract financial, logistical, and administrative confidentiality clauses. For more

information on beyond what is written on the project(s) in this chapter, please kindly contact the respective public and/or private organizations involved in the project(s).

2 The Separation Agreement between Singapore and Malaysia was signed in 1965, which effectively led to the establishment of Singapore as an independent and sovereign country (Ministry of Foreign Affairs, Singapore, 2019). For more information on this agreement, visit the website of the Ministry of Foreign Affairs, Singapore.

3 This sub-section titled "Singspring desalination plant project" is respectively adapted from and/or inspired by the following sources: (Gunawansa, 2010, p. 447; Hyflux, 2019; Kawase, 2018; Keppel Corporation Limited, 2018b; Lee, 2017, 2019; Mukherjee, 2018; The Straits Times, 2018).

4 This sub-section titled "Ulu Pandan NEWater plant project" is respectively adapted from and/or inspired by the following sources: (Gunawansa, 2010, p. 447; Keppel Corporation Limited, 2018a; Keppel Seghers, 2011; Legislative Council of Hong Kong Secretariat, 2016; PUB, 2018).

5 This sub-section titled "Changi NEWater plant project" is adapted from and/or inspired by the following sources: (Asia-Pacific Economic Cooperation, 2014, pp. 1–5; Gunawansa, 2010, p. 448; Sembcorp, 2008, 2009a, 2009b, 2013).

6 This sub-section titled "BEWG-UESH NEWater plant project" is adapted from and/or inspired by the following sources: (Boh, 2017; Ministry of the Environment & Water Resources, 2017; Pablo Publishing Pte Ltd, 2017; PUB, 2014, 2017; Toh, 2017).

7 This sub-section titled "Ulu Pandan wastewater demonstration plant project" is adapted from and/or inspired by the following sources: (Black & Veatch, 2018; Chua, 2018; Global Water Awards, 2018; PUB, 2018; Today, 2015a).

8 This table draws information from the respective sources as previously mentioned in this sub-section.

9 This sub-section titled "Fifth incineration plant project" is adapted from and/or inspired by the following sources: (Gunawansa, 2010, p. 447; Infrastructure Asia, 2019; Keppel Corporation Limited, 2005; Keppel Seghers, 2016).

10 This sub-section titled "ITE college west project" is adapted from and/or inspired by the following sources: (Craft, 2019; Gammon, 2008, 2012; Gunawansa, 2010, p. 448; ITE, 2011; PwC, 2010, 2014).

11 This sub-section titled "TradeXchange project" is adapted from and/or inspired by the following sources: (Chia, 2014; CrimsonLogic, 2014; Gunawansa, 2010, p. 448; Seah, 2011; Taher, Yang & Kankanhalli, 2012).

12 This sub-section titled "Next generation national broadband network project" is adapted from and/or inspired by the following sources: (Gunawansa, 2010, p. 448; IDA, 2010; Singapore Press Holdings, 2008).

13 Table 3.2 is based on information drawn from the sources that are footnoted in the sub-section titled "The DBSS flat projects" in the following pages.

14 This sub-section titled "The DBSS flat projects" was adapted from and/or inspired by the following sources: (CEL Development, 2019; HDB, n.d.; EL Development, 2019; Hoi Hup Realty Pte Ltd, 2019a, 2019b, 2019c; Low Keng Huat (Singapore) Limited, 2019; SAA Group, n.d., 2014; Sim Lian Group Limited, n.d., n.d., n.d.; Singhaiyi Group, n.d.). Given that several of these sources do not indicate a date/year of publication on their post, please refer to the 'References' section for more information about a particular DBSS project. For ease of reference, the title of each DBSS project is italicized.

15 Table 3.3 draws its information from the respective sources that are footnoted in the sub-section titled "Military PPP projects."
16 This sub-section titled "Military PPP training courses" is adapted from and/or inspired by the following sources: (Pilatus Aircraft Ltd, 2018; Australia Defence Magazine, 2006; ST Engineering, 2005, 2008a, 2008b, p. 60).
17 This sub-section titled "NS portal PPP project" is adapted from and/or inspired by the following source: (NCS Group, 2006).
18 This sub-section titled "Rifle range management project" is adapted from and/or inspired by the following source: (Chow, 2010).
19 This sub-section titled "ARTC PPP project" is adapted from and/or inspired by the following sources: (ARTC, 2018; Chan, 2015; Teng, 2015).
20 Table 3.4 draws its information from the sources that are footnoted in the sub-section titled "Medical PPP projects."
21 This sub-section titled "Medical PPP projects" is adapted from and/or inspired by the following sources: (Chan, 2017; Ministry of Health, n.d., 2018; Raffles Medical Group, 2019; Siau, 2017; Singapore Business Review, 2018; Today, 2015b, 2015c).

References

Advanced Remanufacturing and Technology Center. (2018). About ARTC. *Advanced Remanufacturing and Technology Center*. Retrieved July 18, 2019, from www.a-star.edu.sg/artc/About-ARTC/Business-FocusAgency for Science, Technology and Research. (2017). The importance of manufacturing. In *Report on future of manufacturing initiative* (pp. 3–8). Retrieved July 18, 2019, from www.a-star.edu.sg/Portals/81/Data/About.A.Star/SERC-board/Report%20on%20FoM%20Initiative.pdf

Asia-Pacific Economic Cooperation. (2014). Sembcorp NEWater Plant at Changi, Singapore. In *Infrastructure public-private partnership case studies of APEC member economies* (pp. 1–7). Retrieved June 4, 2019, from http://mddb.apec.org/Documents/2014/MM/FMM/14_fmm_019.pdf

Australian Defence Magazine. (2006). News review: Lockheed Martin wins RSAF trainer program | ADM Dec 06/Jan 07. *Australian Defence Magazine*. Retrieved July 17, 2019, from www.australiandefence.com.au/DD630810-F806-11DD-8DFE0050568C22C9

Boh, S. (2017). *$170m fifth Newater plant launched*. Retrieved June 7, 2019, from www.straitstimes.com/singapore/environment/170m-fifth-newater-plant-launched

Black, & Veatch. (2018). Singapore's advanced wastewater treatment technologies wins global recognition. *Eco-Business*. Retrieved June 13, 2019, from www.eco-business.com/press-releases/singapores-advanced-wastewater-treatment-technologies-wins-global-recognition/

The Business Times. (2005, March 8). HDB flats to be designed, built sold like private ones. *The Business Times*, p. 3.

CacheLogic. (n.d.). *Workshop on technical and legal aspects of peer-to-peer television | Trends and statistics in peer-to-peer CacheLogic advanced solutions for P2P networks*. Retrieved July 16, 2019, from https://slideplayer.com/slide/6233177/

CEL Development. (2019). *Belvia (DBSS public housing)*. Retrieved July 17, 2019, from www.celdevelopment.com.sg/sg_sold.phpChan, L. E. (2017). *Calls for stronger partnership between public, private healthcare providers.* Retrieved July 18, 2019, from www.channelnewsasia.com/news/health/calls-for-stronger-partnership-between-public-private-healthcare-9464806

Chan, Y. W. (2015). *A*Star launches Advanced Remanufacturing and Technology Centre.* Retrieved July 18, 2019, from www.businesstimes.com.sg/government-economy/astar-launches-advanced-remanufacturing-and-technology-centre

Channel News Asia. (2019). *Bersatu's Johor chapter to Singaporeans: Ask your government to review water prices.* Retrieved July 7, 2019, from www.channelnewsasia.com/news/asia/johor-assemblyman-singaporeans-government-review-water-prices-11317680?cid=h3_referral_inarticlelinks_24082018_cna

Chia, Y. M. (2014). *PPP: Promised partnerships (can) prosper.* Retrieved July 15, 2019, from www.straitstimes.com/opinion/ppp-promised-partnerships-can-prosper

Chia, Y. M. (2017). *S'pore 'can be world's biggest commodity trading hub'.* Retrieved July 15, 2019, from www.straitstimes.com/business/economy/spore-can-be-worlds-biggest-commodity-trading-hub

Chow, J. (2010). *Civilians to run SAF firing ranges.* Retrieved July 19, 2019, from www.asiaone.com/singapore/civilians-run-saf-firing-ranges

Chua, I. (2018). Ulu Pandan wastewater treatment demonstration plant wins global award. *The Straits Times.* Retrieved June 13, 2019, from www.straitstimes.com/singapore/ulu-pandan-wastewater-treatment-plant-wins-international-award

Chua, M. H. (2005, March 8). Private sector to sell HDB flats: Risky but bold. *The Straits Times,* p. 5.

Craft. (2019). *ITE College West.* Retrieved July 15, 2019, from www.craft-group.com/project/new-ite-college-west-ppp-project/

CrimsonLogic. (2014). *Role of ICT – Learning from Singapore's TradeXchange.* Retrieved 15 July 2019, from www.transportandclimatechange.org/wp-content/uploads/2014/06/Day-3-TradeXchange-Jonathan-Koh.pdf

EL Development. (2019). *Trivelis.* Retrieved July 17, 2019, from http://eldev.com.sg/trivelis/

Fong, H. L. (2013). *Sharing of Singapore's experience in PPP in water infrastructure projects.* Retrieved June 4, 2019, from www.slideshare.net/gwpsea/singapore-27240236?from_action=save

Gammon. (2008). *Gammon Capital wins PPP project in Singapore.* Retrieved July 15, 2019, from www.gammonconstruction.com/en/html/press/press-ff1fcaa1e7514f98801e2613986cb9ed.html

Gammon. (2012). *Institute of Technical Education (ITE) College West Campus, Singapore.* Retrieved July 15, 2019, from www.gammonconstruction.com/en/html/projects/community-development/institute-of-technical-education-college.html

Global Water Awards. (2018). *Water/wastewater project of the year.* Retrieved June 13, 2019, from https://globalwaterawards.com/2018-water-wastewater-project-of-the-year/

Gunawansa, A. (2010). *Is there a need for public private partnership projects in Singapore?* (pp. 440–458). Retrieved December 12, 2018, from www.irbnet.de/daten/iconda/CIB20081.pdf

Housing Development Board. (2018). *DBSS flats.* Retrieved July 17, 2019, from www.hdb.gov.sg/cs/infoweb/residential/living-in-an-hdb-flat/renovation/dbss-flats

Housing Development Board. (n.d.). *List of DBSS sites awarded.* Retrieved July 17, 2019, from www.hdb.gov.sg/cs/infoweb/doc/dbss-master-development

Hoi Hup Realty Pte Ltd. (2019a). *City View @ Boon Keng.* Retrieved July 17, 2019, from http://hoihup.com/portfolio/city-view-boon-keng/

Hoi Hup Realty Pte Ltd. (2019b). *The Peak @ Toa Payoh.* Retrieved July 17, 2019, from https://hoihup.com/portfolio/the-peak-toa-payoh/

Hoi Hup Realty Pte Ltd. (2019c). *Lake Vista @ Yuan Ching.* Retrieved July 17, 2019, from https://hoihup.com/portfolio/lake-vista-yuan-ching/

Hyflux. (2019). *SingSpring Desalination Plant, Singapore.* Retrieved June 4, 2019, from https://hyflux.com/highlights/singspring-desalination-plant-singapore/

Infocomm Development Authority of Singapore. (2008). *Next Generation National Broadband Network for Singapore (Next Gen NBN).* Retrieved July 16, 2019, from www.imda.gov.sg/-/media/imda/files/inner/archive/news-and-events/news_and_events_level2/20080407164702/opcorfp7apr08.pdf

Infocomm Development Authority of Singapore. (2009). *Next Generation National Broadband Network in Singapore.* Retrieved July 16, 2019, from http://mddb.apec.org/documents/2009/TEL/TEL39-LSG-RR/09_tel39_lsg_rr_010rev3.pdf

Infocomm Development Authority of Singapore. (2010). *Building Singapore's next generation nationwide broadband network.* Retrieved July 16, 2019, from www.itu.int/net/wsis/stocktaking/docs/activities/1291981845/Towards%20a%20Next%20Generation%20Connected%20Nation_Singapore.pdf

Infrastructure Asia. (2019). *Keppel Seghers Tuas waste-to-energy plant.* Retrieved July 15, 2019, from www.infrastructureasia.org/en/projects/keppel-seghers-tuas-waste-to-energy-plant

Institute of Technical Education. (2011). *ITE's second comprehensive regional campus – ITE College West – To be officially opened by prime minister Lee Hsien Loong.* Retrieved July 15, 2019, from www.ite.edu.sg/wps/wcm/connect/69ffe780468c2fdfa06ead142ba08ffa/09-11.pdf?MOD=AJPERES&ContentCache=NONE&CACHEID=69ffe780468c2fdfa06ead142ba08ffa

Kawase, K. (2018). *Singapore water company's tap runs dry amid debt crisis.* Retrieved June 4, 2019, from https://asia.nikkei.com/Business/Company-in-focus/Singapore-water-company-s-tap-runs-dry-amid-debt-crisis2

Keppel Corporation Limited. (2005). *Keppel to design and build Singapore's first waste-to-energy plant under public-private partnership initiative.* Retrieved July 15, 2019, from www.kepcorp.com/en/news_item.aspx?sid=1094

Keppel Corporation Limited. (2018a). *Keppel Seghers Ulu Pandan NEWater plant.* Retrieved June 4, 2019, from www.kepinfratrust.com/portfolio/waste-and-water/keppel-seghers-ulu-pandan-newater-plant/

Keppel Corporation Limited. (2018b). *SingSpring desalination plant.* Retrieved June 4, 2019, from www.kepinfratrust.com/portfolio/waste-and-water/singspring-desalination-plant/

Keppel Seghers. (2011). *Keppel Seghers Ulu Pandan NEWater plant.* Retrieved June 7, 2019, from www.keppelseghers.com/en/content.aspx?sid=3027#A2-KSUPNP

Keppel Seghers. (2016). *Waste-to-energy plants – Public private partnership Singapore*. Retrieved July 15, 2019, from https://d2oc0ihd6a5bt.cloudfront.net/wp-content/uploads/sites/837/2016/03/B4_2_TUAN-Loh-Ah_Keppel-Seghers-Engineering-Singapore.pdf

Lee, M. (2017). Foreign buyers eye Hyflux water plant. *The Straits Times*. Retrieved June 4, 2019, from www.straitstimes.com/business/foreign-buyers-eye-hyflux-water-plant

Lee, M. (2019). *The Hyflux story so far*. Retrieved June 7, 2019, from www.businesstimes.com.sg/brunch/the-hyflux-story-so-far

Legislative Council of Hong Kong Secretariat. (2016). *Fact sheet NEWater in Singapore*. Retrieved January 3, 2019, from www.legco.gov.hk/research-publications/english/1516fsc22-newater-in-singapore-20160226-e.pdf

Lin, S. (2019). *Commentary: Beyond scarcity and security, does Singapore need a new water narrative?* Retrieved July 7, 2019, from www.channelnewsasia.com/news/commentary/singapore-water-security-malaysia-conservation-new-narrative-11391186

Low Keng Huat (Singapore) Limited. (2019). *Parkland Residences*. Retrieved July 17, 2019, from www.lkhs.com.sg/portfolio-item/parkland-residences/

Menon, R. (2015). *Ravi Menon: An economic history of Singapore – 1965–2065*. Retrieved July 15, 2019, from www.bis.org/review/r150807b.htm

Ministry of Defence. (2000a). Preface. In *Defending Singapore in the 21st century* (pp. 2–3). Retrieved July 17, 2019, from www.mindef.gov.sg/oms/dam/publications/ebooks/more_ebooks/ds21.pdf

Ministry of Defence. (2000b). Future challenges. In *Defending Singapore in the 21st century* (pp. 7–11). Retrieved July 17, 2019, from www.mindef.gov.sg/oms/dam/publications/ebooks/more_ebooks/ds21.pdf

Ministry of the Environment & Water Resources. (2017). *Speech by Minister Masagos Zulkifli at the official opening of BEWG-UESH NEWater plant at Changi, 18 Jan 2017*. Retrieved June 7, 2019, from www.mewr.gov.sg/news/speech-by-minister-masagos-zulkifli-at-the-official-opening-of-bewg-uesh-newater-plant-at-changi – 18-jan-2017

Ministry of Foreign Affairs, Singapore. (2019). *Water agreements*. Retrieved July 7, 2019, from www.mfa.gov.sg/SINGAPORES-FOREIGN-POLICY/Key-Issues/Water-Agreements (7 July, 2019).

Ministry of Health. (2018). *Community Health Assistance Scheme*. Retrieved July 18, 2019, from www.moh.gov.sg/cost-financing/healthcare-schemes-subsidies/community-health-assist-scheme

Ministry of Health. (n.d.). *About the scheme*. Community Health Assistance Scheme. Retrieved July 18, 2019, from www.chas.sg/content.aspx?id=303

Mukherjee, A. (2018). *Singapore, save your water baby*. Retrieved October 14, 2019, from www.todayonline.com/commentary/singapore-save-your-water-baby

Nakano, T. (2018). *Mahathir picks a new water fight with Singapore*. Retrieved July 7, 2019, from https://asia.nikkei.com/Politics/Malaysia-in-transition/Mahathir-picks-a-new-water-fight-with-Singapore2

NCS Group. (2006). *NCS delivers innovative NS services through public-private collaboration.* Retrieved July 17, 2019, from www.ncs.com.sg/news-room?p_p_id=newsroomportlet_WAR_corpwebportalportlet&p_p_lifecycle=1&p_p_state=normal&p_p_mode=view&p_p_col_id=column-1&p_p_col_count=1&_newsroomportlet_WAR_corpwebportalportlet_newsRoomArticleId=2505&_newsroomportlet_WAR_corpwebportalportlet_javax.portlet.action=viewDetail

National Environment Agency. (2019a). *Waste management infrastructure.* Retrieved 15 July 2019, from www.nea.gov.sg/our-services/waste-management/waste-management-infrastructure/solid-waste-management-infrastructure

National Environment Agency. (2019b). *Waste management.* Retrieved July 15, 2019, from www.nea.gov.sg/our-services/waste-management/overview

National Library Board. (2014). *Introduction of Design, Build and Sell Scheme (DBSS) by HDB.* Retrieved July 17, 2019, from http://eresources.nlb.gov.sg/history/events/4a43df93-2199-4907-b31d-de216e111a22#3

National Library Board. (2015). *National service becomes compulsory.* Retrieved July 17, 2019, from http://eresources.nlb.gov.sg/history/events/debf50d7-d81a-4b31-9c0d-65dd932aab8c

Organization for Economic Cooperation and Development (OECD). (2010). Singapore: Rapid improvement followed by strong performance. In *Strong performers and successful reformers in education: Lessons from PISA for the United States* (pp. 159–176). Retrieved July 15, 2019, from www.oecd.org/countries/singapore/46581101.pdf

Pablo Publishing Pte Ltd. (2017). *Singapore's fifth NEWater plant opens.* Retrieved June 7, 2019, from http://waterwastewaterasia.com/en/news-archive/singapore-s-fifth-newater-plant-opens/707

Pek, S. (2017). *Economic Development Board.* Retrieved July 15, 2019, from http://eresources.nlb.gov.sg/infopedia/articles/SIP_2018-01-08_135544.html

Pilatus Aircraft Ltd. (2018). Pilatus wins key role in Singapore Air Force Basic Wings Course contract. *ASDNews.* Retrieved July 17, 2019, from www.asdnews.com/news-10089/pilatus_wins_key_role_in_singapore_air_force_basic_wings_course_contract.htm

PricewaterhouseCoopers. (2010). *ITE College West, Singapore.* Retrieved July 15, 2019, from www.pwc.com/gx/en/capital-projects-infrastructure/pdf/ite.pdf

PricewaterhouseCoopers. (2014). *Asia's infrastructure trends and case study discussions.* Retrieved July 15, 2019, from www.cpppc.org/u/cms/ppp/201708/141636009jvd.pdf

Public Utilities Board. (2014). *BESIN-UEN Consortium to build second NEWater plant at Changi.* Retrieved June 7, 2019, from www.nas.gov.sg/archivesonline/data/pdfdoc/20140925002/pr20140918_2nd_changi_newater_plant_award_press_release_sally.pdf

Public Utilities Board. (2017). *Singapore's fifth NEWater plant opens.* Retrieved June 7, 2019, from www.pub.gov.sg/news/pressreleases/singaporefifthnewaterplantopens

Public Utilities Board. (2018). *Singapore's advanced wastewater treatment technologies wins global recognition.* Retrieved June 13, 2019, from www.pub.gov.sg/news/pressreleases/singaporesadvancedwastewatertreatmenttechnologieswinsglobalrecognition

Public Utilities Board. (2019a). *About us.* Retrieved June 13, 2019, from www.pub. gov.sg/about

Public Utilities Board. (2019b). *Desalinated water.* Retrieved June 4, 2019, from www.pub.gov.sg/watersupply/fournationaltaps/desalinatedwater

Raffles Medical Group. (2019). *Emergency care collaboration (ECC).* Retrieved July 18, 2019, from www.rafflesmedicalgroup.com/hospital/patients-visitors/ emergency-care-collaboration-(ecc)SAA Group. (2014). *Parkland Residences granted TOP.* Retrieved July 17, 2019, from www.saagroup.com/parkland-residences-granted-top/

SAA Group. (n.d.). *Adora Green.* Retrieved July 17, 2019, from www.saagroup. com/project/adora-green/

SBS Consulting. (2019). *Singapore: The top commodities trading hub in Asia.* Retrieved July 15, 2019, from www.sbsgroup.com.sg/blog/singapore-the-top-commodities-trading-hub-in-asia/

Seah, C. S. (2011). *Public private partnership (PPP) – The Singapore experience.* Retrieved July 15, 2019, from http://siteresources.worldbank.org/INFORMATION ANDCOMMUNICATIONANDTECHNOLOGIES/Resources/D1S3aP3-JosephTeo. pdf

Sembcorp. (2008). *Sembcorp NEWater to start building Changi NEWater plant in April.* Retrieved June 4, 2019, from www.sembcorp.com/en/media/media-releases/energy/2008/february/sembcorp-newater-to-start-building-changi-newater-plant-in-april/

Sembcorp. (2009a). *First phase of Sembcorp Changi NEWater plant completed.* Retrieved June 4, 2019, from www.sembcorp.com/internal_enewsletter/julaug09/ bu_NEWater_Plant.htm

Sembcorp. (2009b). *Sembcorp Changi NEWater Plant begins commercial operations.* Retrieved June 4, 2019, from www.sembcorp.com/en/media/1749/159_ sembcorp_changi_newater_plant_begins_commercial_operations_03aug09.pdf

Sembcorp. (2013). *Sembcorp PUB public private partnership.* Retrieved June 4, 2019, from http://environment.asean.org/wp-content/uploads/2013/07/awgrm/ PPP&O&M-Concession-Mgmt-(Sembcorp).pdf

Siau, M. E. (2017). *Elderly to make up almost half of S'pore population by 2050: United Nations.* Retrieved July 18, 2019, from www.todayonline.com/singapore/ elderly-make-almost-half-spore-population-2050-united-nations

Sim Lian Group Limited. (n.d.). *Centrale 8 At Tampines.* Retrieved July 17, 2019, from www.simlian.com.sg/portfolio/residential/project-for-sale/centrale-8/

Sim Lian Group Limited. (n.d.). *Parc Lumiere.* Retrieved July 17, 2019, from www. simlian.com.sg/portfolio/residential/our-portfolio/parc-lumiere/

Sim Lian Group Limited. (n.d.). *The Premiere @ Tampines.* Retrieved July 17, 2019, from www.simlian.com.sg/portfolio/residential/our-portfolio/the-premier/

Singapore Press Holdings. (2008). *OpenNet is selected to be Singapore's Next Generation National Broadband Network company.* Retrieved July 16, 2019, from https://sph.com.sg/media_releases/664

Singapore Business Review. (2018). *Healthcare spending is shifting from hospital-building to maintenance.* Retrieved July 18, 2019, from https://sbr.com.sg/healthcare/ in-focus/healthcare-spending-shifting-hospital-building-maintenance

Singhaiyi Group. (n.d.). *Pasir Ris One*. Retrieved July 17, 2019, from www.sing-haiyi.com/pasir-ris-one.html

ST Engineering. (2005). *ST Aerospace to provide RSAF with training helicopters worth about $120M*. Retrieved July 17, 2019, from www.defense-aerospace.com/article-view/release/64622/st-wins-$120m-s'pore-training-helo-deal-(nov.-25).html

ST Engineering. (2008a). *ST Engineering's aerospace arm provides RSAF training worth S$105m*. Retrieved July 17, 2019, from www.defense-aerospace.com/articles-view/release/3/97915/st-aerospace-wins-s%E2%80%99pore-af-training-contract.html

ST Engineering. (2008b). ST Engineering at a glance. In *ST Engineering annual report* (pp. 52–88). Retrieved July 19, 2019, from www.stengg.com/media/30113/stear08_full.pdf

The Straits Times. (2018). *Hyflux seeks court protection for debt reorganisation*. Retrieved June 4, 2019, from www.straitstimes.com/business/companies-markets/hyflux-said-to-mull-seeking-court-protection-for-creditor-talks

Taher, M., Yang, Z., & Kankanhalli, A. (2012). Public-private partnerships in e-government: Insights from Singapore cases. In *PACIS 2012 proceedings*. Retrieved July 15, 2019, from https://pdfs.semanticscholar.org/a394/cc2a75809196642bfd1121d02735c5c79df4.pdf

Tay, K. (2015). *Singapore is most vital commodities trading hub in Asia, says IE*. Retrieved July 15, 2019, from www.businesstimes.com.sg/government-economy/singapore-is-most-vital-commodities-trading-hub-in-asia-says-ie

Teng, A. (2015). *JTC and A*STAR launches new facility and centre for remanufacturing technology developments*. Retrieved July 18, 2019, from www.todayonline.com/singapore/jtc-and-astar-launches-new-facility-and-centre-remanufacturing-technology-developments

Today. (2015a). *PUB to build demo plant for testing water reclamation tech*. Retrieved June 13, 2019, from www.todayonline.com/singapore/pub-build-demo-plant-testing-water-reclamation-tech

Today. (2015b). *TODAY Online – Singapore feeling impact of rapidly ageing population*. Retrieved July 18, 2019, from www.gov.sg/news/content/singapore-feeling-impact-of-rapidly-ageing-population

Today. (2015c). *Subsidised rates for patients sent to Raffles Hospital by SCDF ambulances*. TODAY. Retrieved July 18, 2019, from www.todayonline.com/singapore/raffles-hospital-moh-partner-provide-emergency-medical-care-subsidised-rates

Toh, E. M. (2017). *NEWater to meet 40% of S'pore's water needs with fifth plant*. Retrieved June 7, 2019, from www.todayonline.com/singapore/fifth-newater-plant-changi-opens

World Bank. (2019a). *Singapore GDP (current US$)*. Retrieved July 15, 2019, from https://data.worldbank.org/country/singapore

World Bank. (2019b). *GDP per capita, PPP (current international $) Singapore*. Retrieved July 17, 2019, from https://data.worldbank.org/indicator/NY.GDP.PCAP.PP.CD?locations=SG

Yulisman, L. (2018). *Singapore tops new index on investing in education, health*. Retrieved July 15, 2019, from www.straitstimes.com/world/singapore-tops-new-index-on-investing-in-education-health

4 Case studies II

Failure of PPPs in Singapore

Introduction

In Chapter 3, the significant successes that the PPP environment in Singapore has encountered from 2000–2019 were examined. However, during this time period, PPP projects in Singapore have also met with failures for reasons ranging from inadequate financial resources to finishing projects with less than satisfactory project deliverables. Importantly, this chapter reviews six PPP project failures in Singapore from 2000–2019 to elucidate key respective organizational and/or project-specific problems that led to their failure and to contribute new case study-grounded knowledge to the wider PPP governance field about developments and other factors that led to their failure in the Singapore context. Such a contribution can especially encourage current and future PPP scholars to create new conceptual frameworks to better understand the factors and conditions that can lead to a failed PPP project.

Moreover, from the point of view of policy, in pursuing this review, key organizational and/or project management pointers contributing to the failure of the projects are identified for current and future PPP practitioners. In doing so, this chapter hopes that these practitioners will avoid implementing such pitfalls to ultimately minimize the chances of a PPP project failure in the future. Perhaps more crucially, such knowledge can help enhance public trust and confidence in the feasibility of PPP projects delivering effective public services affordably, which is arguably the primary objective of any PPP practitioner in any societal environment.

With these reasons in mind, these reviews will heavily focus on the reasons for the failure of their respective execution phases. By outlining these reasons, this chapter aims to develop, albeit in the Singapore context, case-study driven ideational foundations for the identification of PPP project risk factors that will be addressed in Chapter 5 of this book.

1   Sports services

As the old national sports stadium in Singapore aged, there were calls to upgrade its facilities (Chew, 2016). Therefore, as part of Singapore's Vision 2030 policy, which broadly examined the role that sports can play in, for instance, in enhancing the accessibility of Singapore citizens to new sports facilities and therefore a healthy lifestyle, a plan for the development of a new sports facility that would integrate world-class sports amenities with entertainment facilities was announced in 2001 (Singapore Sports Council [SSC], 2012, p. 4; Tan, 2014). Indeed, the Vision 2030 policy began by posing the question: "How can Sport best serve Singapore in the coming decades?" (Singapore Sports Council, 2019). In response to this policy call, the Singapore government needed the leverage of private-sector know-how on the building and management of sports facilities to effectively build a new Singapore sports hub that would replace the old national stadium. This formed the policy foundation for the launch of the Singapore sports hub project.

Singapore sports hub project[1]

On 29 September 2010, the Singapore sports hub project was launched. In this project, the Singapore Sports Council engaged the Singapore Sports Hub Pty Ltd (a consortium of companies) to design, build, finance, and operate the sports hub over a period of 25 years. Costing 1.33 billion Singapore dollars to build, the sports hub spans 35 hectares and comprises a cluster of sports and entertainment facilities, including but not limited to a national stadium with a retractable roof and a seating capacity of 55,000 together with several retail and dining amenities. However, the execution phase of this project experienced numerous difficulties. Specifically, the consortium ran into funding difficulties and could not complete the project according to the initial timetable. The sports hub was eventually finished on 30 June 2014.

Furthermore, the post-project completion phase was plagued by several technical and management problems. Notably, the hybrid grass pitch, which was a key feature of the sports hub, did not meet the quality standards that were expected by the Singapore Sports Council. This led to complaints from international athletes who used the grass pitch as well as some members of the public in Singapore who questioned the poor accountability and coordination between the Singapore Sports Council and the consortium. As a result, the sports hub had to reschedule events and make urgent repairs to the grass pitch so that the pitch would be ready in time for sporting events. Perhaps most significantly, these developments ultimately created substantial repair costs for the Singapore Sports Hub management team, which were estimated to be at 900,000 Singapore dollars before the inclusion of the goods and services tax.

2   University accommodation services

As the emphasis on innovation and a knowledge-based economy grew in the 1990s (Singapore Management University [SMU], 2011), there was a need to upgrade the university education landscape in Singapore. Examples of this ranged from revising the university curriculum to the expansion of physical facilities such as university student accommodation. Notably, Goh and Tan (2008) summarize the Singapore government's university education reform strategy to kick start Singapore's development into an innovative economy in the 1990s as follows:

> The 1990s saw the consolidation of the government's effort in fine-tuning the tertiary education sector to support its private sector-driven economic modernization strategy. The objective was to create a diversified, flexible tertiary education system capable of producing a highly qualified human resource base. . . . [U]niversities were tasked with training in high-level skills for both the public and private sectors.
>
> (p. 153)

Furthermore, Singapore's university education system is designed to attract academically talented international students to study in Singaporean universities (SMU, 2011). With this inflow of academic talent, an intellectual environment in Singaporean universities that facilitated advanced knowledge transfers between the international and local students would be created. Consequently, this environment would enable universities in Singapore to achieve the task of cultivating high-order skill sets in their students. Upon graduation, these students would constitute a highly skilled workforce that could support Singapore's transition to a knowledge-based economy. Indeed, to successfully create that intellectual environment, the expansion of university accommodation facilities to prepare for higher student intakes in Singapore was required. This requirement laid the developmental groundwork for the National University of Singapore (NUS) university town @ Warren and the SMU hostel projects.

NUS university town @ Warren project[2]

With calls to expand the campus into the Warren area, the project was launched in June 2007. Specifically, the concession company was responsible for designing, building, financing and operating the 6,200-bed student accommodation facility for a period of 25 to 30 years. Worth about 500 million to 600 million Singapore dollars, this project was due for completion before the end of 2010. However, in September 2007, the NUS assumed control of the project, which effectively ended its status as a PPP initiative. Following this cancellation, the project was funded by the NUS through government grants. Importantly, no clear reason has been given for the PPP project cancellation. Nevertheless, according to Gunawansa (2012), it is speculated that:

> as it is a social infrastructure development project, the project proponents found it unviable for development as a PPP, given that administration of the university facilities requires active participation of the public sector, while the revenue for the private sector developer has to be sourced from student fees and other sources of revenue to be generated by the facilities within the University Town. Because the town is an educational institution controlled by the public sector, the private developer's freedom to price the services would have had to be highly regulated, a condition that the private sector developer may have found unfavourable.
>
> (p. 94)

However, the project faced funding difficulties. In response to these difficulties, the NUS management stated that they were "trying to raise funds from donors and not pass on the cost to our students" (Chan, 2010). Hence, the construction of the university town facility was delayed. It was eventually completed and officially opened in 2013.

SMU hostel project[3]

Notably, information on why this project failed is publicly unavailable. Nonetheless, this project has been on hold since 2008. It is likely that the main reasons for this project's suspension are similar to those of the NUS university town @ Warren project. Specifically, given that this project is of a social infrastructural nature, the expectedly heavy involvement of the public sector in this project might have resulted in severe restrictions imposed on the concession company in terms of its freedom to determine pricing charges for its accommodation services. Consequently, this might have made this project too financially risky for the concession company to undertake.

3   Sports entertainment services

In 2008, Singapore hosted one of the rounds of the FIA Formula One World Championship, popularly known as F1 (Lim, 2016). Notably, this F1 round holds the honor of being the first F1 night race in the racing car sports history (Lim, 2016). The hosting of this F1 race in Singapore also had the potential to become an arena in which financial and private wealth management sectors could interact while enhancing related businesses, including but not limited to hotels, nightspots, restaurants and retailers (Singapore Tourism Board, 2011, p. 44). Indeed, the Changi motorsports hub project was:

> a 24/7 hub that would position Singapore to be a regional motorsports destination. It included among other things, an international standard race track able to host global events like the MotoGP and A1 Grand Prix, entertainment complex, showrooms, racing academies, convention halls and even research and development facilities.
>
> (Suhaile, 2015)

Together with the first F1 night race, the Singapore government planned to use the Changi motorsports hub project to establish Singapore as a destination for motorsports fans (Suhaile, 2015). Arguably, this project had the potential to strengthen Singapore's entertainment sector as a whole, which could contribute to its economic development in the long term.

Changi motorsports hub project[4]

SG Changi won the tender bid to construct the permanent motor race track in March 2009. The public institution involved in this project was the Singapore Sports Council, and the project was estimated to cost 380 million Singapore dollars. However, SG Changi was investigated by Singapore's Corrupt Practices Investigations Bureau (CPIB) for irregularities in the tender. This caused the project investors to withhold funding from SG Changi. The investors also required SG Changi to be cleared by the CPIB before they would release the project funds. Consequently, SG Changi failed to pay the cost of piling work for the Changi Motorsports Hub, which was worth 50 million Singapore dollars.

With this failure to deliver payment, the construction of the motorsports hub stopped, and SG Changi eventually missed key project deadlines. In December 2011, the Singapore Sports Council terminated the project partnership with SG Changi. Following this, in October 2014, SG Changi paid 6.9 million Singapore dollars to the piling contractor company, CS Construction and Geotechnic (CSCG), a wholly owned subsidiary of CSC Holdings. Notably, the group chief executive officer of CSC Holdings commented on SG Changi's role and debt payment in the failed project:

> [the debt payment] was a long wait, but it looks like Christmas came early for us this year. To be fair, I think SG Changi did their best, but they were caught during a time when the economy was not good and had difficulty raising funds.
>
> (De Cotta, 2014)

Moreover, SG Changi had to bear the cost of conducting a request for information exercise in 2012 to identify whether the project should be released again for tender. In 2012 there were more futile attempts to revive the project, but the Singapore Sports Council finally decided to give up on pursuing it altogether in 2013.

4 Public transport services

Singapore is an island city/state with a geographical area of approximately 718 square kilometres and a population of 5.5 million (Chang & Phang, 2017). In 1975, Singapore became the first city worldwide to introduce a road congestion pricing system, and in 1990, it introduced a motor vehicle ownership quota (Phang, 2014). This resulted in the rising cost of owning and operating a private vehicle in Singapore and, in turn, led the majority of the population to utilize the public transport system as a means of getting around.

Therefore, fare affordability and the quality and reliability of public transport facilities were crucial to the majority of the Singapore population and were given much policy attention (Chang & Phang, 2017). Indeed, a major public transportation system in Singapore is the Mass Rapid Transit (MRT) railway network. The Singapore government heavily invested in the MRT's initial rail infrastructure and its operating assets (Chia, 2016).

The first lines were opened in 1987; however, the 1996 transport White Paper recognized the potential financial stresses on the MRT operators when the MRT network was fully state-owned (Chia, 2016). It was hoped that with the privatization of most of the MRT system, it would be exposed to greater market competition, which could arguably enhance its reliability and fare affordability. These potential benefits formed the policy motivation for the Singapore government's pursuit of the MRT PPP initiatives.

MRT PPP initiatives[5]

The MRT network in Singapore transitioned from a being a fully state-owned system to one that sees the ownership of infrastructure being separated from rolling stock and operations. Under this new system, the Singapore government owns the railway infrastructure assets, whereas the private sector finances and owns rolling stock, operates the MRT train services and maintains the railway infrastructure. In 1998, the operating assets of the MRT's north-south and east-west lines were transferred by the Singapore government to the Singapore Mass Rapid Transit (SMRT) Corporation Limited. Notably, SMRT was listed on the Singapore stock exchange in 2000. Also, in 1999, SBS Transit was awarded the tender to operate the MRT's northeast line. However, in 2002, an individual with retail industry experience and no previous background in operating urban rail transit systems was appointed SMRT's chief executive officer. This appointment led to:

> SMRT's new focus on conversion of previously underutilised spaces at stations to retail and commercial spaces. The result was a significant increase in profits from rental of station properties for SMRT.
>
> (Chang & Phang, 2017)

In addition, Singapore's rapid population increase from 4.4 million in 2006 to 5.2 million by 2011 resulted in overcrowding in MRT trains and unexpectedly longer waiting times during peak hours. These situations caused much unhappiness among the commuters. On 15 December 2011, SMRT had its first major breakdown, which affected about 127,000 commuters. Two days later, a second major breakdown caused Singapore's prime minister to launch a Committee of Inquiry (COI) to investigate the causes and emergency readiness of SMRT to handle service breakdowns. Those two breakdowns led to the resignation of the chief executive officer who had no previous experience in operating urban rail systems. Importantly, the COI report also found that there were shortfalls in the Land Transport Authority (LTA)'s regulatory supervision of SMRT's rail maintenance and the capital improvement of infrastructure.

Despite increased government attention to enhancing MRT's network capacity and enhancing its rail reliability since these incidents of service breakdown, there were 14 further major service disruptions in 2014 and 29 service disruptions in 2015. In 2016, the Singapore government announced that its LTA would pay SMRT 1.06 billion Singapore dollars for its rail operating assets and SMRT was delisted from the Singapore stock exchange. This delisting effectively meant that the Singapore government resumed full ownership of SMRT.

5 Water services

Similar to the water projects reviewed in Chapter 3, the motivations for pursuing the Tuaspring integrated water and power plant project as a PPP was to ensure a reliable, efficient, and sufficient supply of potable water in Singapore given its limited natural water resources. However, the PPP project eventually failed. Details of this failed project are presented in the following paragraphs.

Tuaspring integrated water and power plant project[6]

For this project, the main objective was to engage a private entity to design, build, own, and operate a desalination and power plant. The desalination plant was built to supply the Public Utilities Board with potable water for

25 years. The power plant was constructed to supply electrical energy to the desalination plant, and any excess electrical power produced was to be fed to the power grid in Singapore. The public organization involved was the PUB, and the private organizations involved were Tuaspring and Hydrochem (both are subsidiaries of Sembcorp Industries). The project was launched in June 2010, and the desalination plant was completed in 2013, with the power plant being completed in 2014. The estimated project worth of this project was about 1.05 billion dollars.

During this project's launch phase, Hydrochem was responsible for constructing the integrated water and power plant. In July 2011, this project's execution phase began with the construction of the integrated plant. The water desalination plant was designed to produce 318,500m³ of potable water for the PUB daily with the use of advanced ultra-filtration technology for the pre-water treatment process.

This technology uses fewer chemicals and less energy than regular water desalination plants by utilizing a two-stage seawater reverse osmosis (SWRO) process followed by the re-mineralization of the water, after which the water is supplied to the PUB. The power plant was designed to produce 411 megawatts of electricity and was equipped with turbines, generators, and a plant control system.

The plant was connected to the power grid in Singapore in 2015. However, during the project's post-project completion, Hyflux ran into deep financial troubles when it failed to restructure its debt, with its liabilities amounting to 2.95 billion Singapore Dollars in 2018.

The PUB terminated its water purchase agreement with Tuaspring on 17 May 2019.

Following this termination, the PUB took over the desalination plant from Hyflux at zero dollars on 18 May 2019. This move was made to safeguard Singapore's water security. Moreover, the PUB retained employees with the relevant operational skillsets to run the desalination plant and has supported a smooth takeover of the plant.

Notes

1 This sub-section titled "Singapore sports hub project" is adapted from and/or informed by the following sources: (Chia, 2014; Gunawansa, 2010, p. 449; Nair, 2016; Singapore Sports Hub, 2019; Tan, 2014).

2 This sub-section titled "NUS university town @ warren project" is adapted from and/or informed by the following sources: (Chan, 2010; Gunawansa, 2010, p. 449, 2012, p. 94; Ling, 2016; NUS, 2019; Prime Minister's Office, 2013).

3 This sub-section titled "SMU hostel project" is respectively adapted from and/or informed by the following source: (Chia, 2014). Notably, Mr. Paul Wong, a senior partner at Dentons Rodyk and Davidson LLP, which is a limited liability partnership firm that is registered in Singapore, was responsible for the handling of the SMU hostels project case (Dentons Rodyk & Davidson LLP, 2019). Readers who

are interested to find out more about this project may approach Dentons Rodyk and Davidson LLP or SMU for more information.

4 This sub-section titled "Changi motorsports hub project" is adapted from and/or informed by the following sources: (Chia, 2014; De Cotta, 2014; Suhaile, 2015).

5 This sub-section titled "MRT PPP initiatives" is adapted from and/or informed by the following sources: (Chang & Phang, 2017; Chia, 2016; Gomez-Ibanez & Goh, 2016).

6 This sub-section titled "Tuaspring integrated water and power plant project" is respectively adapted from and/or inspired by the following sources: (Lee, 2019; Seow, 2019; Verdict Media Limited, 2019).

References

Chan, R. (2010). *NUS UTown widens campus living options.* Retrieved August 7, 2019, from www.asiaone.com/News/Education/Story/A1Story20100330-207515.html

Chang, Z., & Phang, S. Y. (2017). *Urban rail transit PPPs: Lessons from East Asian cities.* Retrieved August 10, 2019, from https://ink.library.smu.edu.sg/cgi/viewcontent.cgi?article=3097&context=soe_research

Chew, H. M. (2016). *NDP 2016 brings back fond memories of old National Stadium: 5 things you may remember.* Retrieved August 4, 2019, from www.straitstimes.com/singapore/ndp-2016-brings-back-fond-memories-of-old-national-stadium-5-things-you-may-remember

Chia, J. (2016). *S'pore's rail industry reinvents itself with new financing scheme.* Retrieved August 10, 2019, from www.todayonline.com/commentary/spores-rail-industry-reinvents-itself-new-financing-scheme

Chia, Y. M. (2014). The sorry saga of the grass pitch at the Sports Hub has put public-private partnerships in the spotlight. But such PPPs can prosper with the right structure. *The Straits Times.* Retrieved August 4, 2019, from www.straitstimes.com/opinion/ppp-promised-partnerships-can-prosper

De Cotta, I. (2014). *SG Changi settles motorsports hub debts.* Retrieved August 10, 2019, from www.todayonline.com/sports/motor-racing/sg-changi-settles-motorsports-hub-debts

Dentons Rodyk, & Davidson LLP. (2019). *Paul Wong.* Retrieved August 7, 2019, from https://dentons.rodyk.com/en/paul-wong

Goh, C. B., & Tan, W. H. L. (2008). The development of university education in Singapore. In S. K. Lee, C. B. Goh, B. Fredriksen, & J. P. Tan (Eds.), *Toward a better future: Education and training for economic development in Singapore since 1965* (pp. 149–166). Washington, DC: The World Bank.

Gomez-Ibanez, J. A., & Goh, B. (2016). *Restructuring mass transit in Singapore (Teaching case).* Cambridge, MA: Kennedy School of Government, Harvard University.

Gunawansa, A. (2010). *Is there a need for public private partnership projects in Singapore?* (pp. 440–458). Retrieved December 12, 2018, from www.irbnet.de/daten/iconda/CIB20081.pdf

Gunawansa, A. (2012). The use of the public private partnership concept in Singapore. In G. M. Winch, M. Onishi, & S. Schmidt (Eds.), *Taking stock of PPP and PFI around the world* (pp. 90–98). London: Certified Accountants Educational Trust for the Association of Chartered Certified Accountants.

Lee, M. (2019). *The Hyflux story so far*. Retrieved June 7, 2019, from www.businesstimes.com.sg/brunch/the-hyflux-story-so-far

Lim, S. K. (2016). *Inaugural Formula One Singapore Grand Prix*. Retrieved 10 August 2019, from http://eresources.nlb.gov.sg/infopedia/articles/SIP_1392_2009-11-19.html

Ling, H. (2016). *The problem with PPPs in Singapore*. Retrieved August 7, 2019, from https://thediplomat.com/2016/09/the-problem-with-ppps-in-singapore/

Phang, S. Y. (2014). Managing private vehicles in Asian cities. In *Conference Proceedings of Asia Public Policy Forum 2014: Urban transport and land use in rapidly growing Asian cities*. Ho Chi Minh City, Vietnam, June 5–6.

Nair, S. (2016). *Sports Hub drops claims over $900k damage to National Stadium pitch*. Retrieved August 4, 2019, from www.straitstimes.com/singapore/sports-hub-drops-claims-over-900k-damage-to-national-stadium-pitch

National University of Singapore. (2019). *Third Master Plan ('90s to 2000s)*. Retrieved August 7, 2019, from https://uci.nus.edu.sg/physical-planning/campus-master-plan/third-master-plan-90s-to-2000s/

Prime Minister's Office. (2013). *Speech by Prime Minister Lee Hsien Loong at the official opening of University Town*. Retrieved August 7, 2019, from www.pmo.gov.sg/newsroom/speech-prime-minister-lee-hsien-loong-official-opening-university-town

Seow, J. (2019). *PUB takes over Tuaspring desalination plant from Hyflux*. Retrieved June 7, 2019, from www.straitstimes.com/business/pub-takes-over-tuaspring-desalination-plant-from-hyflux-0

Singapore Management University. (2011). *What the future holds for higher education in Singapore*. Retrieved August 7, 2019, from www.smu.edu.sg/perspectives/2012/06/26/what-future-holds-higher-education-singapore

Singapore Sports Council. (2012). Executive summary. In *Vision 2030: Live better through sports* (pp. 4–6). Retrieved August 4, 2019, from www.myactivesg.com/~/media/Corporate/Files/About/Vision%202030/LiveBetterThroughSportsV2030SteeringCommitteeReport2012.pdf

Singapore Sports Council. (2019). *Vision 2030*. Retrieved August 4, 2019, from www.sportsingapore.gov.sg/about-us/vision-2030

Singapore Sports Hub. (2019). All venues. In *About Us*. Retrieved August 4, 2019, from www.sportshub.com.sg/about

Singapore Tourism Board. (2011). Tourism sector performance. In *i'mpact Singapore Tourism Board annual report 2010/2011*. (pp. 34–47). Retrieved August 10, 2019, from www.stb.gov.sg/content/dam/stb/documents/annualreports/i'mpact2010-2011.pdf

Suhaile, M. (2015). *End of the road for motorsports hub*. Retrieved August 10, 2019, from https://sg.news.yahoo.com/end-road-motorsports-hub-070657900.html

Tan, S. Y. (2014). *National Stadium*. Retrieved August 4, 2019, from https://eresources.nlb.gov.sg/infopedia/articles/SIP_1441_2009-02-09.html

Verdict Media Limited. (2019). *Tuaspring desalination and integrated power plant*. Retrieved June 7, 2019, from www.water-technology.net/projects/tuaspring-desalination-and-integrated-power-plant/

5 Conclusion

Lessons learned from practice

1 The gap between theory and practice

In the previous two chapters, this study has closely explored and investigated PPP projects carried out between 2000–2019. This enquiry looked at 32 successful PPP projects and six failed ones in diverse service (industry) areas. Through comprehensive and focused research, there was some evidence found to support the answer to the following central question: What drives (or hinders) the effective management of PPPs? An investigation of the existing literature on PPPs found positive and negative factors pertaining to their success to be either 'critical success factors' (CSFs) or 'critical risk factors' (CRFs), respectively. These factors seemed quite complex and multidimensional.

By comparing successful cases with failed cases, this study found that that a total of 38 PPP cases have commonly revealed that the Singapore government has been increasingly dependent on diverse private stakeholders across organizational boundaries and has moved toward greater project efficiency over the past two decades. In other words, the adoption and operation of PPPs in Singapore has gained political and top-management support. The main reasons why the government has harnessed expertise, capital finance, and other resources (i.e., the know-how, information, and personnel resources) of the private-sector actors seems to not only be able to provide innovation-driven high-quality public services to its citizens but also to achieve long-term economic productivity. In the pursuit of such major aims, the Singapore government has continued to proceed with PPP projects related to essential infrastructure policy (e.g., transport), social welfare policy (e.g., medical services and housing), environmentally friendly energy-saving policy (e.g., wastewater recycling and the use of rooftop solar power), and other future industries (e.g., R&D, ICT, and engineering), mostly in service areas that require asset-specific investments from the private sector, such as a large amount of money and manpower (labor intensive). As Chieh (2017) and Hodge and Greve (2007) have insisted, it seems that through PPPs, the government could have a greater capacity to spend on 'core' functions and other policy priorities because there is a substantial fall in the financial burden shouldered by the public partners.

In recognition of this general observation, this study further attempted to specify the CSFs derived from various PPP cases in Singapore. The following CSFs embedded in successful PPP cases are listed below:

1   Clearly defined roles and responsibilities of the public and private parties involved,
2   Both public and private parties agreeing on a common operational and execution style to achieve the project objective(s),
3   Both public and private parties sharing a sustained commitment to achieve the project goal(s),
4   Demonstrated relevant technical competency of the concession company,
5   Healthy finances of the concession company (the so-called financially strong private consortium) in the long term, and
6   Clear lines of communication (channels) between the management body and the 'workers on the ground' in the concession company when executing a project.

Taken together, the evidence seems in line with Han's (2016) argument that "[a] successful PPP would have clearly defined roles and risks, open channels of communication and healthy relationships between public and private stakeholders."

On the other hand, the evidence found in this study shows that government agencies engaging in the PPP projects often might find themselves in a dilemma. This dynamic situation occurs due to (un)expected managerial risks associated with internal and external circumstances. According to Baker (2016, p. 438), internal and external risks that may induce additional or hidden transaction costs during the PPP contract period can be differentiated at large as: (1) financial and operational risks including cost overruns/waste, fraud, abuse, and corruption, and (2) political and regulatory risks including environmental disturbances or fluctuations of demand (e.g., unfavorable public sentiment against the building/renovation of one infrastructure facility). Of course, the size and scope of these risks may vary across service (industry) areas, as well as from country to country. But it should be noted that large-scale PPP projects are likely to have higher levels of such risks as compared to small-scale ones, regardless of a country's economic status (developed versus developing countries) (Coghill & Woodward, 2005; Landow & Ebdon, 2012). Acknowledging this, this study attempted to focus on internal and external risks and found that most of these issues appeared to arise during the execution phase of PPP projects.

As noted earlier in previous chapters, there is a general understanding that PPPs help achieve "better value for money (VFM)" and provide better service outputs/outcomes to fulfill citizens' increasing needs and expectations. Yet, the failed PPP cases explored here obviously indicate a discrepancy between the widely accepted efficiency rationales (e.g., cost savings) underlying PPPs and real-world conditions. They seem to be at odds with traditional public choice theory and transaction cost theory. Specifically speaking, sometimes PPP projects incur contract (tender) failure, which, in turn, may lead the public partners to take over the unsatisfactory performance of targeted services (e.g., poor quality of services provided or socially unacceptable service outputs/outcomes) and bear hidden costs (e.g., additional repair costs afterwards). Poorly performing PPP projects eventually made the Singapore government return to self-operation (in-house [direct] production) of the services once a PPP project was found to fail to achieve the mutual goal(s) that the public- and private-sector actors had agreed upon.

In line with this perspective, the study found that the main cause behind PPP failure across different service areas seems to be the private sector's (consortium's) funding difficulties. In practice, many private partners tended to struggle with debt/liability issues because they could engender loss of the funds initially invested (Hwang et al., 2013). For example, in cases where several investors decide to withhold funds from the consortium in the middle of project operation, funding problems are more likely to occur. Given this, it is reasonably expected that stakeholders in the PPP project will eventually face time delays in construction/building, while missing the due/deadline promised in a contract. In turn, the return on investment (ROI), known as profit/revenue gains, also will be postponed. Besides, another notable factor derived from the failed cases of PPPs in Singapore is that private partners also could encounter unexpected risks (i.e., inflexible and rigid ways in which the public sector works). As a result, private partners are likely to be in trouble coordinating and sharing risks and accountabilities with the public counterparts for service outcomes. The following CRFs embedded in the failed PPP cases are listed below:

1   A lack of stable financial capacity of the private partners during the execution period of a project,
2   Inadequate technical competency or the absence of relevant technical competency of the key decision-makers in the concession company,
3   Lack of understanding of project objective(s) by either, or both of the public and private partners,

4   Poor coordination of risk allocation/sharing between the main stake-holders,

5   Inadequate experience or lack of experience in PPP projects by either or both the public and private partners, and

6   The presence of strict or excessive rules and regulations by the public works.

2   Three main pillars of successful PPPs

After closely analyzing CSFs and CRFs stemming from successful and failed cases in PPPs in Singapore, as well as those found in the existing literature, this study found variations in the common factors associated with the success-failure continuum of PPPs. First, the following three main pillars are believed to enhance the operation of PPPs, especially in regards to massive infrastructure projects: (1) establishing strong, effective, and consistent institutional and legal environments, (2) investing in government in-house capacity, and (3) ensuring clear and agreeable risk allocation and sharing (see Figure 5.1). These pillars have been inspired by Brown and Potoski's (2003) argument that "[t]he success or failure of any alternative service delivery arrangement likely depends on how well governments can manage the entire contracting process" (p. 153). We believe that these pillars will

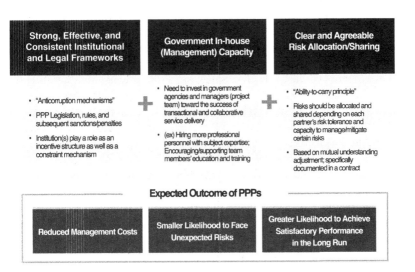

Figure 5.1 Three Main Pillars of Successful PPPs

Source: Authors' own elaboration

commonly help reduce management costs throughout the entire PPP process. Governments intending to develop effective PPP projects are strongly recommended to incorporate the pillars into the project requirements and standards for better future practices.

The first significant pillar of successful PPPs is strong, effective, and consistent institutional and legal environments (e.g., state law or ordinance). In support of Yang et al.'s (2013) argument for the necessity of 'anticorruption mechanisms' *per se* in the PPP projects, this study views that the operating environment of PPPs needs to be open, fair, and transparent and sometimes coercive (e.g., enforcement of supervision, performance evaluation, and auditing).

Notably, institutions are likely to act as a mediating force between legal requirements (e.g., rules and subsequent formal sanctions/penalties) and the incentives and responses of related actors. Some of the leading scholars in the field of political science and economics (e.g., North, 1990; Ostrom, 1990; Williamson, 1985) have long envisioned the role of institutions as an incentive structure as well as a constraint mechanism affecting (shaping) actors' decision-making and behaviors, including social exchanges and interactions. Aligning with this viewpoint, this study posits that governments can curb self-interested private partners who opportunistically exploit the government's information advantages and even public managers who pursue their own interests rather than the goals of agencies and public interest, by developing and implementing clear and strong institutions and legislation for the effective management of PPP projects. In doing so, it is reasonably expected that the first pillar helps the public sector to minimize unexpected risks, thereby reducing its physical and financial burdens. Further, it can lower transaction costs (e.g., monitoring costs).

As mentioned earlier in the Singapore PPP system, there has been a noticeable absence of frontline organizations (perhaps independent project teams) as well as a lack of related laws (legal framework) that can link the effective micro-management of PPP projects (Zen & Regan, 2014). Accordingly, this mechanism seems to be worthy of special attention for the success of PPPs in the long run. Of course, as in the PPP Handbook developed by the Ministry of Finance (MOF, 2012), Singapore, it is also highly recommended to have more decentralized project teams with a senior executive (leader) per team with experience in performing the work and some internal and external (legal, technical, and financial/auditing) advisory groups per each PPP project within the public partner.

Next, the second pillar recounts the widely cited observation that higher levels of government in-house (management) capacity matter for enhancing the operation of PPPs. Recent research gives further confidence in this normative expectation. For instance, in the context of contracting out, Kim (2017) noted that "[c]ontractors . . . sometimes are likely to encounter uncertainties and respond to contingencies. This case may occur when government agencies conduct unfair bidding processes or minimal monitoring due to the lack of management capacity" (p. 757). In the PPP setting, Yang et al. (2013) stated that "[t]he government (agencies), whether it participates as a partner or regulator, must possess the appropriate aptitude in terms of expertise, knowledge, and information, as well as the means to acquire the appropriate aptitudes if it does not yet possess them" (p. 303).

In a situation in which governments lack or fail to maintain or improve their capacity, one would expect that the governments would easily become dependent on the private partners (known as contractors or external service providers) or sometimes are "captured" by the counterparts (e.g., for more information, see Carr & Brower, 2000; Kettl, 1993; Stigler, 1971). Therefore, it might be challenging for them to hold contractors accountable for expected outcomes (Kim, 2015). In the existing literature on PPPs or governments contracting out tasks, many scholars have agreed with this point, arguing that the appropriate expertise and resources of government agencies and managers can play a role as a potential answer to the salient challenges of the PPP management and performance (e.g., Bae & Joo, 2016; Brown & Potoski, 2003; Kim, 2017, 2019; Soomro & Zhang, 2015; Yang et al., 2013). This means that the public-sector actors who are engaged in long-term ongoing partnering relationships may have enough reason to devote their efforts toward the success of transactional as well as collaborative service delivery, for example, through intensive monitoring (including financial oversight), fair evaluation, mutual understanding, frequent communication, and feedback or information sharing with private-sector actors (Kim, 2015, 2017). In this context, Cohen and Eimicke (2008) pointed out the role of responsible managers, stating that "[p]ublic managers must become effective contract managers and need to learn how to: (1) find out what their contractors are doing, (2) develop and implement systems of contractor incentives, (3) get a fair price for services, and (4) develop the skills needed to negotiate performance-based contracts" (p. 123). In addition, from the organizational perspective, government agencies (perhaps project teams) need to invest their time and resources in achieving effective management of PPP projects, for example, by hiring more professional personnel with subject expertise and encouraging/supporting their managers' (team members') education and training.

The last pillar points to the importance of clear and agreeable risk allocation and sharing between the two main partners of PPPs. To facilitate effective PPP management in the short run and to further achieve satisfactory performance of PPPs in the long run, such risk allocation work possibly should be made at the early stage of PPP projects (Hwang et al., 2003). In this way it is more likely to achieve value for money (VFM) in PPPs in that an appropriate allocation of risks between partners can minimize the likelihood of renegotiation and legal proceedings due to conflicts of interest (Marques & Berg, 2011; Roehrich, Lewis, & George, 2014).

However, it should be noted that project-oriented risks have often been seen as underestimated and allocated to PPP participants without deeper consideration of each actor's resources and capabilities (Ng & Loosemore, 2007). Besides, most of the project-oriented risks are likely to be transferred to the private-sector actors (e.g., consortium) in practice (Warsen et al., 2019). However, this might not always be a desirable idea because this could entail increased transaction costs (e.g., due to project delays or conflicting interests) (Ng & Loosemore, 2007) and "affect the progress or future participation of private investors in PPP projects" (Osei-Kyei & Chan, 2015, p. 1342).

More importantly, to date, many PPP scholars in the public administration and policy area have recognized the need for risk allocation and sharing, however, their discussions have been generally fragmented with a low level of consensus, and even their evidence and suggestions seem largely descriptive rather than prescriptive. Singapore PPPs are not an exception in this respect. For example, according to the PPP Handbook of MOF (2012, p. 6), the Singapore government has simply recommended that the public partner (government agencies) will be responsible for political and regulatory risks, whereas the private partner will bear risks pertaining to design, construction, and financing. No clear requirements nor specific categories of actual and potential risks stemming from PPPs have been discussed in the Singapore PPP system.

In acknowledging this challenge, this study suggests that the so-called ability-to-carry principle should be widely adopted. In other words, as noted by Warsen et al. (2019), "[i]n PPPs, risks should be allocated to the partner who is best able to carry or mitigate risks" (p. 380) because each partner will have different levels of risk tolerance and varying degrees of capacity to manage certain risks (Bing et al., 2005; Wang & Zhao, 2018). Bearing in mind that the optimal allocation and transfer of risks can vary depending on service (industry) areas, there is a need for mutual understanding and consistent adjustment between the two main partners, and the acceptable degree of this flexibility should be negotiated prior to the actual awarding of a contract (tender). Moreover, this agreement over optimal allocation and transfer of risks should be clearly and specifically documented and bound in a legal contract (tender) of PPPs.

3 The future of PPPs: lessons for scholars and practitioners

Notably, due to the growing popularity of PPP projects around the globe over the last few decades, a huge amount of literature about PPPs has flourished beyond the area of merely public administration and policy. Yet, compared to Western cases, including Europe and the United States, to date, limited attention has been paid to Asian cases of PPPs. In particular, there has not been any comprehensive, chronological research of PPPs in the Singapore context. This study has attempted to fill the knowledge shortfall in this area by closely exploring operationally successful and also unsuccessful cases of PPPs in Singapore.

In order to more deeply probe this issue, this evidence-seeking exploratory study not only introduced under-examined (or newly found) evidence about PPP projects in a broader array of public service areas over the period 2000–2019 but also discussed critical success factors (CSFs) and critical risk factors (CRFs) that explicitly and implicitly reveal the possibility of a disconnection between theory (e.g., traditional public choice theory and transaction cost theory) and practice. The findings of this study, though limited, help both public and private-sector partners to better understand the important factors (conditions) leading to successful win-win PPP operations, including the roles and responsibilities of each partner involved. In doing so, this study also provides valuable information for potential service suppliers (among investors and developers in the private market) who are willing to participate in PPP projects in Singapore.

In today's complex and changing times, PPPs still appear to remain an attractive alternative to the public management (financing) of major infrastructure projects, mainly due to their expected VFM and high-quality services or performance (Soomro & Zhang, 2015). As noted in the several failed cases of PPPs explored in this study, however, a PPP is not a panacea for all major city projects (Han, 2016). The effective development of PPPs indeed depends upon a variety of organizational, institutional, relational, and environmental conditions and factors embedded in the management process of PPPs.

Given this, the main lessons from the case studies of PPPs in Singapore are suggested as follows: First, government agencies (project team) and managers need to be subject themselves to the demanding requirements of PPPs to ensure the effective management of projects both in the areas of efficiency and accountability. In the words of Yang et al. (2013), "[t]o facilitate smooth PPP project management, a participating government must demonstrate credibility as a responsive and responsible party in all contractual relations" (p. 303). In addition, the public partners are advised to collaborate with private counterparts whose expertise and motivation to innovate is needed and should be based on periodic two-way communication and sharing of feedback with each other. In doing so, governments can reduce hidden transaction costs and risks as well as attract more private equity (capital) financing in the long run.

Meanwhile, within the success-failure continuum of partnering relationships, there is still much to learn about PPPs. Especially, there has been a lack of in-depth discussion about causes behind PPP failures, as Roehrich et al. (2014) argued. Therefore, future research should continue to pursue new evidence and find more validated lessons pertaining to the topic using comparative case studies. In other words, scholars and practitioners need to scrutinize the factors that facilitate or sometimes tackle the success of worldwide PPPs at the national level as well as at the local level. Beginning with a comprehensive literature review pertaining to CSFs and CRFs of PPPs, they may consider comparing (or recounting) the widely cited previous observations (the factors) with the evidence found in this study. Another possible starting point might be based on a cross-national comparison in a same-service area (regarding one specific infrastructure). For this, scholars should compare a set of factors emerging from similar cases in at least two different countries, merge the differentials, and further offer additional detailed insights about feasible strategies and the institutions needed to move toward successful PPP projects along with maintaining satisfactory performance in the long run.

In addition, for more convincing analyses and arguments, further investigation is needed to test the perceptions of both public and private partners participating in current PPP projects regarding the conditions in which two main actors are most likely to share risks, benefits, and responsibilities in an effective and accountable manner. In doing so, researchers will be enabled to gain the depth of detail of the subject in a way that represents the reality of the situation over the rhetoric surrounding it. Presumably, the private-sector actors can provide different stories and ideas regarding CSFs and CRFs from another angle. For example, it is possible that private partners will be more critical of their counterparts (here, government) with regard to the government's PPP management process and capacity (e.g., issues of ambiguous regulations, too much restriction and red tape, unclear project targets, or weak leadership in the public agency). As such, it is worth conducting focused research through focus group interviews with PPP participants across service areas or survey questionnaires and comparing their (perhaps somewhat polarized) views across different sector actors.

Last, to paint a more complete picture of successful PPPs along with supporting satisfactory performance in the long term, future studies should develop performance dimensions and with measurement indicators that might be universally applicable to all PPP projects. Ultimately, this scholarly effort is expected to contribute to the existing literature in that it may help build a comprehensive model (framework) for the effective management of PPPs.

Although the evidence found in this study cannot be generalized to all services or to all governments and is still very preliminary, it is hoped that this book will help readers to make greater sense of the particularities and complexities of PPPs in Singapore as well as beyond the Singapore context. The authors believe that the analytical approach and arguments posed will not only serve as a useful departure point for future research but also will guide current governments and policymakers who are operating PPPs but still struggling with visible and invisible managerial challenges or just planning to proceed with PPP projects.

References

Bae, Y., & Joo, Y.-M. (2016). Pathways to meet critical success factors for local PPPs: The cases of urban transport infrastructure in Korean cities. *Cities, 53,* 35–42.

Baker, N. B. (2016). Transaction costs in public-private partnerships: The weight of institutional quality in developing countries revisited. *Public Performance & Management Review, 40*(2), 431–455.

Bing, L., Akintoye, A., Edwards, P. J., & Hardcastle, C. (2005). The allocation of risk in PPP/PFI construction projects in the UK. *International Journal of Project Management, 23*(1), 25–35.

Brown, T. L., & Potoski, M. (2003). Contract-management capacity in municipal and county governments. *Public Administration Review, 63*(2), 153–164.

Carr, J. B., & Brower, R. S. (2000). Principled opportunism: Evidence from the organizational middle. *Public Administration Quarterly, 24*(1), 109–138.

Chieh, L. W. (2017). *Policy analysis: Singapore's public-private partnerships for cybersecurity in the critical infrastructure sectors – challenges and opportunities.* Singapore: Lee Kuan Yew School of Public Policy at the National University of Singapore. Retrieved June 27, 2019, from https://lkyspp.nus.edu.sg/docs/default-source/case-studies/singapore-s-public-private-partnerships-for-cybersecurity-in-the-critical-infrastructure-sectors_challenges-and-opportunities.pdf?sfvrsn=9c38960b_2

Coghill, K., & Woodward, D. (2005). Political issues of public-private partnerships. In G. Hodge & C. Greve (Eds.), *The challenge of public-private partnerships: Learning from international experience* (pp. 81–94). Cheltenham, UK: Edward Elgar.

Cohen, S., & Eimicke, W. (2008). *The responsible contract manager: Protecting the public interest in an outsourced world.* Washington, DC: Georgetown University Press.

Han, L. (2016). The problem with PPPs in Singapore: The decision to scrap a PPP for Changi Airport Terminal 5 reveals the difficulties of making this model work.

The Diplomat. Retrieved June 28, 2019, from https://thediplomat.com/2016/09/the-problem-with-ppps-in-singapore/

Hodge, G., & Greve, C. (2007). Public-private partnerships: An international performance review. *Public Administration Review, 67*(3), 545–558.

Hwang, B., Zhao, X., & Gay, M. (2013). Public private partnership projects in Singapore: Factors, critical risks and preferred risk allocation from the perspective of contractors. *International Journal of Project Management, 31*(3), 424–433.

Kettl, D. F. (1993). *Sharing power: Public governance and private markets*. Washington, DC: The Brookings Institution.

Kim, S. (2015). *Toward financially effective contract management: Comparing perceptions of contract managers in the public and private sectors* (Doctoral dissertation, Rutgers, The State University of New Jersey). Retrieved from https://rucore.libraries.rutgers.edu/rutgers-lib/47684/PDF/1/play/

Kim, S. (2017). Lessons learned from public and private contract managers for effective local government contracting out: The case of New Jersey. *International Journal of Public Administration, 40*(9), 756–769.

Kim, S. (2019). Understanding and operationalizing financial accountability in government contracting systems. In A. Farazmand (Ed.), *Global encyclopedia of public administration, public policy, and governance*. Cham: Springer.

Landow, P., & Ebdon, C. (2012). Public-private partnerships, public authorities, and democratic governance. *Public Performance & Management Review, 35*(4), 727–752.

Marques, R., & Berg, S. (2011). Public-private partnership contracts: A tale of two cities with different contractual arrangements. *Public Administration, 89*(4), 1585–1603.

Ministry of Finance (MOF), Singapore. (2012). *Public private partnership handbook: Version 2*. Retrieved June 25, 2019, from www.mof.gov.sg/Portals/0/Policies/ProcurementProcess/PPPHandbook2012.pdf

Ng, A., & Loosemore, M. (2007). Risk allocation in the private provision of public infrastructure. *International Journal of Project Management, 25*, 66–76.

North, D. C. (1990). *Institutions, institutional change, and economic performance*. Cambridge, UK: Cambridge University Press.

Osei-Kyei, R., & Chan, A. P. C. (2015). Review of studies on the critical success factors for Public-Private Partnership (PPP) projects from 1990 to 2013. *International Journal of Project Management, 33*, 1335–1346.

Ostrom, E. (1990). *Governing the commons: The evolution of institutions for collective action*. Cambridge, UK: Cambridge University Press.

Roehrich, J. K., Lewis, M. A., & George, G. (2014). Are public-private partnerships a healthy option? A systematic literature review. *Social Science & Medicine, 113*, 110–119.

Soomro, M. A., & Zhang, X. (2015). Roles of private-sector partners in transportation public-private partnership failures. *Journal of Management in Engineering, 31*(4), 04014056.

Stigler, G. J. (1971). The theory of economic regulation. *The Bell Journal of Economics and Management Science, 2*(1), 3–21.

Wang, Y., & Zhao, Z. J. (2018). Performance of public-private partnerships and the influence of contractual arrangements. *Public Performance & Management Review, 41*(1), 177–200.

Warsen, R., Klijn, E. H., & Koppenjan, J. (2019). Mix and match: How contractual and relational conditions are combined in successful public-private partnerships. *Journal of Public Administration Research and Theory, 29*(3), 375–393.

Williamson, O. E. (1985). *The economic institutions of capitalism: Firms, markets, relational contracting.* New York, NY: Free Press.

Yang, Y., Hou, Y., & Wang, Y. (2013). On the development of public-private partnerships in transitional economies: An explanatory framework. *Public Administration Review, 73*(2), 301–310.

Zen, F., & Regan, M. (2014). ASEAN public private partnership guidelines. *Economic Research Institute for ASEAN and East Asia.* Retrieved July 6, 2019, from https:// asean.org/storage/2016/09/Public-Private-Partnership-in-South-East-Asia.pdf

Index

Printed in the United States
by Baker & Taylor Publisher Services